BEND IT LIKE YOU:

PERSONAL STORIES OF RESILIENCY AND PERSEVERANCE FROM PEOPLE JUST LIKE YOU

NANCY NG

Bend It Like You: Personal Stories of Resiliency and
Perseverance From People Just Like You

ISBN 978-0-9881219-1-1

Publisher: Nancy Ng (Edmonton, Alberta, Canada)

Book Cover design: Cover Creator

Printer: Kindle Direct Publishing (formerly CreateSpace)

Editor: Norma Jean (NJ) Brown

Proofreader: Wei Wong

Contact information:
Email: Nancy@NancyNgSite.com
Website: NancyNgSite.com

CTN

For when the night is falling
you cannot find a friend
if you feel your tree is breaking
just then
you got the music in you
don't let go
you've got the music in you
one dance left
this world is gonna pull through
don't give up
you've got a reason to live
can't forget
we only get what we give

**"You Get What You
Give", by the New
Radicals**

Table of Contents

Introduction

In this book, I hope to draw attention to the stigmatized views surrounding mental health and mental illness and the negative effects of these stereotypes. I hope my book will encourage more people to seek help, especially if they wouldn't have before. Because personal mental health stories are not often detailed in most books or in mental health literature, my hope is that this book will help further raise awareness of the importance of talking about the taboo topics of mental health and mental illness and debunk any stereotypes associated with them.

I believe that encouraging more conversations about mental health and mental illness will bring to light the importance of talking about these two concepts. These discussions have been suppressed for far too long, and we've lost far too many lives because of the suffocating silence. As a social-issues writer, these themes affect me daily and are important for me to speak about in my writing. I hope this book will add to the current social discourse and increase awareness of mental health and mental illness issues, even as the writing of it helps me develop my social-activist voice.

I found the people whose stories are featured in this book either through social media, referrals by others, the University of Alberta Alumni magazine, or amongst people I already knew. I interviewed most of them face-to-face (some through FaceTime), and others submitted their answers via email. I used whatever method was most comfortable for them. Though they knew they were part of a project, and were being interviewed with focus on 16 specific questions, I spoke to the eight individuals just like a friend having coffee with them on a Sunday afternoon would do. They are from various backgrounds, reflecting different cultures and roles in society: included are parents, the educated, the disabled, the young, and the transgender population, all with messy and complicated lives. Most importantly, they are real. Just like you.

This book is a social documentary of people's lives and mental well-being. I'm not a doctor, a therapist, or a counsellor of any sort. What I am is a social-issues or social-activist writer. Everyone around me (family, friends, strangers, co-workers, acquaintances) seems to be going through mental health issues; it's an epidemic loaded with stigma that prevents a lot of people from seeking help. I hope this book and these stories will encourage people to seek help, and, if not, at least help them feel less alone. I think a lot of us feel we're the only ones feeling a certain way.

I am humbled and inspired by each and every one of the eight individuals in this book, what they went (or are going) through, and the wisdom they each radiated. Each of these stories is ongoing, but, most importantly, their stories do not define these individuals. A tree in the eye of a storm may bend and break, but it may also bend and resist—just like you. Life is not a sitcom that ends happily-ever-after after 30 minutes. Just like the eight people in this book, we are all a work in progress. Many of these people are in mid-transition, searching and hoping, bending (but not breaking) against the winds of life.

In this book, I provide only a brief background about resiliency, perseverance, and mental health because I didn't want this book to be academic. I didn't want to spend a whole bunch of time researching online or in the library (does anybody use the library anymore?) to write this book. I was far more interested in hearing people's stories from the people themselves. And no purely academic book can come close to capturing the complexity of one's life or mind.

I had to step away from working on this book every time I finished an interview. Each story was heavy for me, and I felt it. If I'm in excellent shape, it's only because I walked a lot in the last few years. Walking helps me clear my head, decompress, sort things out, and try to make sense of things. I became more sensitive, sympathetic, and empathetic when I heard about the struggles of others. These stories also stripped away some of my past judgements.

This book is not organized by personality type, particular backgrounds, or experiences. Rather, this book uses people's stories to demonstrate why we need to share our own mental health stories; it also shows how we are more alike than different. That we are all vulnerable, regardless of background or where we are in our lives. That we can no longer suffer in silence and need to reach out for help. That we are not alone. The moment we share our story is the beginning. Being vulnerable and telling our stories is when the healing begins. By telling our stories, we will bend, but we will not break. No more silence! Share your story to end the stigma of mental illness. No one is an island. By helping each other, simply by sharing our stories, we all rise together for the well-being of others and for ourselves.

The first part of my book provides information about resiliency, perseverance, mental health, and the stigmas and stereotypes of mental health. It then trails into eight chapters of personal experiences from eight brave individuals. The book ends with an appendix of the 16 questions I asked the individuals during their interviews. Being able to see these questions may help the reader understand the interviewees' problem-solving skills, whether they built social connections, and how they maintained dialogue with others.

Resiliency

"At the heart of resilience is a belief in oneself – yet also a belief in something larger than oneself" (Estroff Marano, 2003, para. 2).

Whether large scale (e.g. terrorist attacks or tornadoes), or simply minor (e.g. missing your train), your response to setbacks and challenges can play a huge role in your long-term psychological journey. Resilient people are able to keep their cool and cope with adversity. According to Cherry's article, The Importance of Resilience (2019), "Resilient people are able to utilize their skills and strengths to cope and recover from problems and challenges" (Para. 4).

Whether experiencing financial hardships, medical emergencies, marital problems, or natural disasters, resilient people face them head-on. This is not to say they don't experience the distress, grief, or anxiety that others do; they just address these curve balls with strength and growth with a view of the glass as being always half full. When the less resilient are faced with disappointment, unhealthy choices may follow. As a result, they may experience more psychological distress.

Resilient people "understand that setbacks happen and that sometimes life is hard and painful. They still experience the emotional pain, grief, and sense of loss that comes after a tragedy, but their mental outlook allows them to work through such feelings and recover" (Cherry, 2019, para. 6). Whether facing Hurricane Katrina or coping as a survivor of 9/11, the resilient remain strong when facing unimaginable tragedy. They move forward and try to help others affected by similar circumstances. They not only survive, but also prosper emotionally as human beings.

What characteristics do resilient people share?

- They have the social support of family and friends who lift them up in times of need.
- They hold positive views of themselves and what they're capable of.
- Their plans are realistic, and they stick to them.
- They have an internal sense of control.
- They are good communicators.
- They see themselves as fighters, not as victims.
- They are in touch with their emotions and manage them well.

"Resilience is what gives people the psychological strength to cope with stress and hardship. It is the mental reservoir of strength that people are able to call on in times of need to carry them through without falling apart" (Cherry, 2019, para. 1).

Perseverance

Perseverance and resiliency go hand in hand.

"Perseverance cultivates a sense of purposefulness that can create resilience against or decrease current levels of major depressive disorder, generalized anxiety disorder, and panic disorders" (American Psychological Association, 2019, para. 1).

Looking on the bright side of tragedy creates a sense of meaning and understanding. According to the article "Perseverance toward life goals can fend off depression, anxiety, panic disorders: Looking on the bright side also acts as a safeguard, according to 18-year study," individuals suffering from depression, anxiety, or panic disorders get stuck in the cycle of negative thought patterns and behaviors. More often than not, this makes them feel even worse. The authors of the article, Hani Zainal and Michelle G. Newman, used data from 3,294 adults who were studied over 18 years. The data was collected three times: 1995-1996, 2004-2005, and 2012-2013. Results from the data show that more optimistic individuals had a greater reduction in depression, anxiety, and panic disorders. The study found that you can improve your mental health by increasing resiliency and optimism.

"Aspiring toward personal career goals can make people feel like their lives have meaning. On the other hand, disengaging from striving toward those aims or having a cynical attitude can have high mental health costs" (American Psychological Association, 2019, para. 7). Don't give up! Doing so may provide temporary relief, but it will likely increase regret and disappointment. Stick with your goals even when you hit a wall; this will generate a more positive mood and a sense of purpose.

Mental Health

Mental health is not only about avoiding mental illness. It's also about balancing your work, health, and relationships. We can't be truly healthy without being mentally healthy. How we act and interact with, and feel and think within, our environment is a big part of mental health. "Mental health is about realizing our potential, coping with the normal stresses of life, and making a contribution to our community" (Canadian Mental Health Association, 2016, para. 1). When you are mentally healthy, you're thriving in your life, you're not trying to achieve perfection, and you're living well despite the valleys in your life. Mental health is not necessarily about the absence of mental illness. There are people with mental illness who are healthy, and there are physically healthy people who don't have good mental health.

Not everybody's road to mental health will be the same. But the tools we can all use to move toward a healthy mindset and lifestyle are closer than you think.

Here are some tools from the Canadian Mental Health Association website, which suggests what can work for you as you move towards a healthier life:

1. Put your self-esteem on a pedestal. Self-esteem is about highlighting your good and bad qualities, embracing them for what they are, forgiving yourself, and looking ahead to self-improvement. Self-esteem is about focusing on what makes you unique and following your goals without comparing yourself to others. Take the road least taken, and your self-esteem will reach for the stars.

How do you do this? You can begin by asking yourself what you do best. How would your friends describe you? Caring? Practical? What are the areas you feel you can improve in or have the most difficulty with? Impatience? Keep in mind that everybody has strengths and weaknesses. You're not the only one. You're a 3D, multifaceted, complex person. Propel your confidence to the stratosphere by working on your weaker areas and continuing to take pride in your strengths.

2. Build and maintain your support networks. These people (family, friends, other supporters) can offer you support on so many different levels, such as providing alternate points of views and emotional or practical support. Keep these people close to you, and you will have a healthier life.

    How do you do this? Spend lots of time with the most important people in your life. These are the positive people who support and uplift you. They're your biggest cheerleaders in life! You can laugh with them and be serious with them as well. Stay away from emotional vampires filled with negative energy. They can do nothing for you but lead you down the road of despair and hopelessness.

3. Get involved in your community. Everybody needs to feel like they have a purpose and most people want to make a difference in someone else's life. Get involved in groups or organizations that make you feel connected to others. You'll meet and connect with people who share similar interests. You'll build your confidence and learn new skills while meeting other like-minded people.

    How do you do this? If you love babies, volunteer to cuddle and rock premature babies at your local hospital. If you love seniors, volunteer at your local senior's home. Perhaps you can share your social-media skills with a not-for-profit organization or your juggling skills with your local Boys and Girls Club. Or how about serving as a board member for your favourite non-profit organization?

4. Change what you can, and let go of what you can't. Accidents, conflicts, or unexpected life changes will happen, and they'll happen to everyone. It's an inevitable part of life. The key is to have a toolkit ready that prepares you for life's challenges and surprises. Having resiliency in your toolbox will help you decipher what you can control and change and what you can't control or change; it also helps you see the blessings in your life. Having resiliency includes things like possessing good problem-solving skills, being proactive, balancing wants and needs, and having good people in your life.

   How do you do this? Think about the resiliency tools you have in your life. Do you have friends and/or family who are there for you and are good influences? Are you good at problem solving? What worked for you in the past? Did helping others help you in the past? Keep this list close to you for when you encounter another of life's challenges. This list is also a reminder of what you can add to shore up future support.

5. Check in on how you're feeling. As nice as it would be, you can't be happy all the time. Nobody can. Feeling the whole range of different emotions is part of being human. Respect for ourselves and others involve expressing our emotions in a healthy way. Bottling up emotions or lashing out isn't healthy for anybody. We need to recognize and be conscious of our emotional well-being, think about how it affects our behavior, correct our action when our emotions go off kilter, and embrace our emotions, even the bad ones. Tomorrow will be a better day!

   How do you do this? Ask yourself what makes you happy, sad, or angry? What brings you peace? Take note of how to best deal with your various moods. Exercise can help with anxiety, for example. Or build a collection of inspirational quotes for when you need a picker-upper or some encouragement. Have funny DVDs ready for when you need a laugh. Listen to your favourite music; it has the power to lift you up or bring your peace.

6. Don't forget about your spiritual well-being. Spiritual well-being may include religion, but, for many of us, it's more about how we feel about ourselves. It's about what we value, what our purpose is, and living with integrity. It's about knowing there's something bigger than ourselves, building connections with others, and overcoming adversity.

   How do you do this? Carve out a physical space and time for some alone time. Try inhaling while counting to four, then exhale and repeat. Or go dancing, ice climbing, hiking, or shooting hoops. Whatever works for you!

Stereotypes and Stigma of Mental Illness

More often than not, mental illness is seen as dangerous or uncomfortable. This results in stigma and discrimination through exclusion within social situations or in employment against those suffering from mental illness. According to Link, Cullen, Struening, and Shrout's study (as cited in Davey, 2013), "**Social stigma** is characterized by prejudicial attitudes and discriminating behavior directed towards individuals with mental health problems as a result of the psychiatric label they have been given. In contrast, **Perceived stigma** or **Self-stigma** is the internalizing by the mental health sufferer of their perceptions of discrimination." A study by Perlick, Rosenheck, Clarkin, Sirey et al. (as cited in Davey, 2013) revealed that "a perceived stigma can significantly affect feelings of shame and lead to poorer treatment outcomes."

Who holds stereotypes and stigmas around mental illness? According to a study by Crisp et al., (2000), Moses, (2010), Wallace, (2010) (as cited in Davey, 2013), almost everyone. We may know someone with mental illness, have family members with mental illness, or have had experience with mental illness personally. Shockingly, "Mental health stigma is even widespread in the medical profession, at least in part because it is given a low priority during the training of physicians and GPs" (Wallace, as cited in Davey, 2013, para. 4).

What factors cause this stigma? In his article, Davey explains that early beliefs about mental illness characterized it as demonic. In contemporary times, the entertainment media perpetuates the stigma and stereotypes of mental illness. For instance, the cinematic portrayal of a schizophrenic is often stereotyped with false information, including causes and treatments. People with mental illnesses are more often than not negatively and unfairly portrayed as being unavoidably violent, homicidal, or suicidal.

What are the social effects of this stigma around mental illness? "Exclusion, poor social support, poorer subjective quality of life and low self esteem" (Livingston & Boyd, as cited in Davey, 2013, para. 7). This stigma also affects treatment outcomes and effective recovery from mental health problems (Perlick, Rosenheck, Clarkin, Sirey et al., as cited in Davey, 2013, para. 7) as well as poorer employment success and increased social isolation (Yanos, Roe & Lysaker, as cited in Davey, 2013, para. 7).

Mental health is like any other health problem, such as diabetes, cancer, or heart attacks. Yet, it is looked upon differently because of the stigma attached to it. This stigma perpetuates the negative attitudes and negative behaviours directed toward people with mental health problems: They aren't normal; they're not like us; they caused their own problems; they can get over their problems if they only try harder. Stigma can also prevent people from getting and keeping a job, from having a safe place to live, from getting proper health care and support, and from being accepted within their social circles.

The Centre for Addiction and Mental Health (CAMH) suggests seven ways we can reduce stigma surrounding mental illness:

- Know the facts. Learn the facts instead of the myths.
- Be aware of your own prejudices, and change the way you think. People exist as unique human beings, not as labels or stereotypes.
- Choose your words carefully. Be accurate and sensitive with your words when talking about people with mental health problems. For instance: "A person with schizophrenia," rather than "a schizophrenic," which suggests that the illness is the entirety of the person suffering from it.
- Educate others. Spread facts and positive attitudes about people with mental illness. Challenge the myths and stereotypes of mental illness that are presented by the media.
- Focus on and applaud the positive contributions to society that people with mental illness have made. Again, their health problems are not their entire identity.
- Support people. Treat them with respect and dignity. Support their choices and encourage them to get well.
- Include everyone. People with mental health issues have as much of a right as everyone else to jobs, housing, health care etc. We violate human rights when we don't include them.

The Fire Within

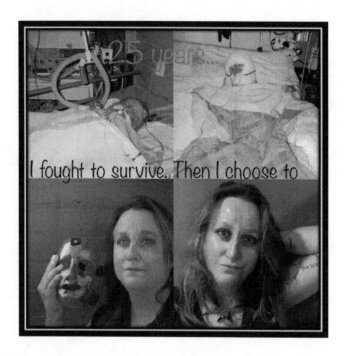

Believe it or not, it took awhile (okay, months) for me to build up the courage to message Joy Zylstra to ask if I could interview her for this book. One day, in a Venezuelan restaurant (of all places), I was feeling brave, so I took the plunge and messaged Joy on Facebook. She messaged me back not long after that, and I was elated. I first read about Joy and her story on the "Humans of Edmonton Experience" Facebook page. She has quite a presence on the page, and I love how she writes the stories of other people's struggles. The stories are honest, gritty, and raw, yet respectful. Her personal story also struck me enough for me to reach out to her because I could see something that radiated within her, and it's nothing short of extraordinary.

Joy is the middle child of Jean and John Rawson and comes from a large family of seven children. When Joy was nine years old, she and her family went to visit the children's aunt and uncle at their cabin in British Columbia. Joy and two of her sisters stayed in the guest cabin. There was no electricity, and the only way to get light in the cabin was to light a candle. "On July 25, 1993, I was bored," Joy says. "I was only nine. Everyone else was over by the main cabin, just relaxing. So I went to the guest cabin to play with my toys. I do remember walking to the cabin, and I had this big feeling in my stomach, and it felt weird. I knew I wasn't hungry because we'd just eaten, and to this day I do think it was God saying 'stop and turn around!'" Joy walked into the cabin and remembers smelling something. She noticed the valves on the propane stove were turned on, but there were no flames. She shut it off and didn't think anything of it. She then went to light the candle to see what she was doing, and her life changed forever.

"Next thing I knew, I opened my eyes and saw the carpet with millions of sparks everywhere. I wasn't on fire; nothing was. But in two seconds, a flash fire happened. It was equivalent to 2500 degrees Fahrenheit. So it became incredibly hot in just two seconds. It was a log cabin, and all the logs lifted up. My sister's sleeping bag was blown up with the logs, and they fell back down. The roof went up and came down sideways. Shelves fell. And I was in the middle of it all."

Joy wasn't in any pain, but she was scared, and she screamed. Everybody heard the explosion, but they didn't know what it was. Joy's father and uncle came running and their only mission became to get help for Joy while Joy's mom stayed back with the rest of the family. In 1993, there was no cellphones, and they also didn't have a house phone to call an ambulance. The cabin was in the middle of nowhere. Fortunately, Joy's uncle was able to get her to an ambulance center more quickly than an ambulance could have gotten to her.

"I do remember my dad holding me. He had cut off all my clothes. Wrapped me up in towels drenched with mountain water. And I remember him holding me on the drive, asking me 'how are you feeling?' I said, 'I'm tired, and I'm really hot, but I'm also really cold.' I said, 'I just want to sleep.' He kept saying, 'Nope, nope, you can't go to sleep.' He knew enough to know that if I went to sleep, I might not wake up because I would go into shock."

They finally arrived at the ambulance center. Joy's father was holding her and pounding on the door at the same time. By this point, the gravity of the situation was hitting her father pretty hard. He was in shock too, but he stayed strong for Joy. "He's my hero. He literally saved my life," Joy says. He also knew his daughter was in good hands when he handed her over to the paramedics, and that was all that mattered. Joy was flown to Vancouver via helicopter. Her father stayed with her while her uncle went back to the cabin where the rest of the family was.

At the Vancouver General Hospital, doctors told her father that Joy might not survive that night. Her entire body was swollen. Her head was the size of two basketballs, and slits were cut into her bandaged body to let the fluid out. "The last memory I have of Vancouver was them taking my earrings out and giving them to my dad. He put them in his left shirt pocket. I don't have any other memory of Vancouver."

By the time Joy's mother made it to the hospital, six hours had passed from the time of the explosion—six hours of not knowing whether Joy was going to survive or not. It was probably the longest six hours of Joy's mother's life. Fortunately, Joy survived the night. But she was burnt very badly. Vancouver General Hospital couldn't help her further because the burn unit there was full. Vancouver General Hospital then called a hospital in Calgary, and their burn unit was also full. They also tried the University of Alberta (U of A) Hospital in Edmonton, which was also full. However, fortunately, the U of A Hospital never refuses anyone. They transferred their healthiest burn patient into the Intensive Care Unit to open up a bed for Joy.

Joy and her mother were flown to Edmonton. Her father went back to get the rest of the kids and family and drove from British Columbia to Camrose (their home) in half the time it normally would have taken (24 hours). Joy's father didn't know if Joy was going to survive, so the adrenaline kicked in. "I remember him saying, 'I dare any cop to pull me over,'" Joy says. In Edmonton, the U of A Hospital plastic surgeon in the burn unit, Dr. Ted Tredget, helped Joy immensely. Joy felt he also saved her life. "That was where my parents were told I suffered from 2nd and 3rd degree burns to 45% of my body," she says.

If it weren't for her family, Joy wouldn't have made it through the struggles ahead. "My family is absolutely amazing," Joy says. "I'm never alone. When I was in the hospital, I always had my mom and dad there, and then my siblings came to visit me as well as aunts, uncles, neighbours, and schoolmates. As for the physical healing process, I did lose a lot of friends. I was in Grade 4. They were just kids. I don't hold any grudges, but a lot of kids didn't want to be my friend." Back then, Joy's physical appearance was hard to look at. Her skin was purple and red. It looked bloody, and she was bald. She also had to wear a mask. It was a very hard time for Joy. "I looked like a freak. And kids are scared of what they don't know, right?"

As a teenager, Joy felt her parents were coddling her too much. But in hindsight, she sees that they were just loving her and taking care of her as best as they could. They treated all of the children the same. Despite the love from her family, Joy's mental health was crumbling. "I was suicidal," she says. "I attempted suicide three times as a teenager. It was a friend who helped me get help. But over the years, my parents have been my biggest supporters in everything I did. And I definitely, over the years, know who my true friends are."

Throughout the mental pain that Joy went through, she's had people tell her to just "get over it." If only it were that easy. The explosion "literally changed my entire life," Joy explains. "The way I look and everything. I sometimes refer to it as dying in that cabin and being reborn. I know I'm not the same person I would be if I never got burned." No doubt, Joy is a stronger person. She feels she's become more compassionate. Even though she was nine years old when the explosion happened—almost 25 years ago this year (2018)—it still impacts her today as an adult. She knows what she experienced is no more important than someone else's experience: "I want to hear people's stories. I want to hear what they struggled with, what hurt them and how they got through it."

It's taken some time, but Joy has a more positive view of herself now. She loves her scars and how they look. But she hasn't always been this kind to herself. Her confidence comes from years of hard work on herself, therapy, and those closest to her, such as her family and her closest friends. They remind her that she's a strong person. Since she's had children (two daughters, Ciara and Sahtaysha, and a son, Paxton), Joy is adamant about being a good role model for them. "I asked myself what I'd be teaching them if I looked down on myself, or treated myself badly, or didn't hold my head high." Growing up, the stares from people tanked Joy's self-esteem. After a lot of hard work to regain that self-esteem, she was able to hold her head up instead of looking down in shame. She doesn't notice the stares as much as she used to, even though people still stare at her. The stares don't hurt her anymore, whereas she used to struggle with them to the point that she didn't want to be seen in public. Now, she says, "I don't think there's anything I can't do." You go girl!

I don't know about you, but I think Joy is incredibly inspirational. "Hell will freeze over before I let my scars get in the way of anything," she says. "There are scars all over my body, but they will never get in my way." The physical pain was always there while she was growing up, but it never robbed Joy's spirit as she got older: "I do remember crying to my mom as a teenager. 'What am I going to do? There's nothing for me in life. What am I doing to do?' I remember her just holding me and saying, 'Joy, you can be the next Oprah if you want to.'" Oprah, being an African-American, overweight woman with her own television talk show shattered the norm then and continues to do so today. And so can Joy.

Though Joy developed nerves of steel resiliency as she got older, controlling her feelings and impulses have been a struggle for her: "I'm on anti-depressants and anti-anxiety medication. Before taking the medication, the people closest to me unfortunately got the brunt of it all. If something was bothering me mentally—if my husband didn't sweep the floor, for example—I would lash out and make it such a bigger deal than it really was because of what was bothering me in my head, and I couldn't control it. But it's much better now." For the most part, Joy feels she's in control of her life and the choices she makes. Her life isn't perfect, but whose life is?

I asked Joy what some of her problem-solving skills are. "I think I definitely put my ideas out there to my closest friends and family now. I'm afraid of putting some things out there publicly and asking for help because I'm afraid of people judging me. I know who in my circle I can talk to about whatever, knowing they won't judge me. My best friend, for instance, will be honest with me and say, 'Joy, you're being an idiot.' You know, she'll be honest with me." Joy can also depend on her father. He always says to her, "Victims don't exist," and tells Joy that she's a survivor. He has always been Joy's rock.

At the time of the accident, because Joy was so young, she did feel like a victim. Understandably, she felt helpless and sorry for herself. For years, she kept asking, "Why me, why me, why did it happen to me?" This has changed. "Now, today, I have no regrets. I wouldn't change a thing," she says. Joy was very close to her grandmother, so when her grandmother passed away, it hit Joy really hard. She did feel helpless in that situation. Or if something bad happens to her children, Joy still goes through cycles of "Why me; why is this happening?" After going through a lot of tears, anger, and frustration, Joy sits down and talks with the person who she feels can best help her at that moment in time, whether it's her husband, her best friend, her dad, or her mom. Joy says a good night's sleep also helps immensely. It helps her bounce back, awakening the next day revitalized in her quest to find solutions that will make things, including her feelings, better.

Negative experiences are definitely blessings in disguise. Joy has a website called "scarrednotbroken.com." She also has a Facebook page, Instagram page, and a YouTube video. She shares people's life experiences and their stories. Traumatic events such as a gay person coming out of the closet, addiction, a car accident, or abuse are just a few examples. "I just want to help people," Joy says. "With all the pain that I've gone through, both in the hospital and in later years with mental anguish, the worst feeling was the feeling of being alone. I knew I wasn't the only burned person in the world. I was never physically alone. I always, always had somebody with me. But I still felt alone. I felt nobody knew what I was going through, and it sucked. That's why I started "scarrednotbroken.com." I want somebody to hear my story and think, "If she can do it, I can do it."

Joy has used several coping mechanisms that she's happy to share. Joy was raised in a strict Catholic family, and there were lots of prayers for Joy when the accident happened. But while lying in her hospital bed, nine-year-old Joy was cursing God. It was like, "What the fuck!?" Joy says. Her parents were pillars in Joy's life when she needed someone to lean on or to help her make sense of the situation. Her mother was there Monday to Friday, and her father was there on the weekends. Most importantly, they never babied Joy.

When Joy returned home from the hospital, covered in medical gauze and wearing a mask and with limited mobility, her parents knew best by giving her the time and space to do things on her own and to let her develop a sense of independence. They let her figure things out on her own, but also let her know they were there if she needed them. "No pain, no gain," her father used to say to her. Not babying Joy helped her heal faster not only physically but also mentally: "I'm not ever going to be the type of person who relies on somebody else to do things for me or to make things better for me. Years later, with the mental anguish that I was going through, I thought drugs, alcohol, and sex would help. It made it worse, obviously. Ultimately, it was when I had my daughter that I turned everything around. How I thought about things, how I looked, and how I felt about myself. I didn't want her to ever grow up hating herself. How could I teach her that if I didn't believe in myself?"

Does Joy cope with stress in healthy ways now? Sometimes she'll call a friend or her family when dealing with a lot of stress. "I wish that I could just go have a bath and relax," she says. "And I can have a bath and relax normally, but when I'm stressed over something, it doesn't work. I'm a control freak too. So if something is going on, I want it fixed now. 'Let's get a plan, let's get it done, and let's get it fixed.' It's all I can think about," she says.

How do her family and friends cope with their own stress? Joy's mom copes with life's struggles by having tea, but Joy says she doesn't really know how other family members and friends cope with stress. "If it works for her, that's great," she says about her mom. "Again, I'm too impatient. I can't shut my brain off. You know, if I'm stressed about something and if I were to sit down and have a cup of tea like my mom does, okay great, but I'd still be thinking about the problem the whole time." Fair enough!

Though we all try to avoid negative experiences, Joy believes it's important to have these negative experiences because they can help us grow as individuals. "I'm not a practicing Catholic anymore, but I am spiritual," Joy says. "I do have a relationship with God, and I believe in him. We talk. From lying in a hospital bed and cursing him to being a depressed and suicidal teenager crying in my bed, scratching at my face, and praying, 'Just let me wake up without my scars.' Now I'm very proud of them. One thing my mom has always told me is that God answers every prayer; sometimes it's just not the answer you're looking for. So even though I obviously didn't hear his answers to my prayers in the last 25 years, life has shown me that there's a reason for everything. I couldn't imagine not being burned. I know if I weren't burned, I wouldn't have the three kids I have. I wouldn't have my husband; I might be married to someone else and have different kids. But I love my life and the people I've met and the person I've become. I don't believe God intended for this accident to happen, but it did. So I think he said, 'Alright, you'll get through it.' He gave me the strength, or helped me find the strength and confidence, to be the woman that I am today. It took a long, long time, but ..."

It will be 25 years this year (2018) since the accident. "I don't let myself feel sorry for myself," Joy says. "But I do allocate myself one day per year, if needed, to sit and cry about what happened, because it did suck, you know? Maybe my life would be better if I wasn't burned? I don't know. It sucked. Everything I went through sucked. I think by giving myself that one day, usually around the anniversary of my accident, not usually on the same day of the accident, but usually around, I spend time on my own to just cry it out."

After a good cry, Joy feels better. "I just wanna be by myself. But I only allow myself that one time a year because life's too short—there's nothing you can do about it. What's done is done, and I'm not going to feel sorry for myself, and I'm not going to drive the pity train. But I do think that it's healthy to just let myself have that once-a-year moment. Again, it's only if it's needed, and I haven't needed to do it every year."

Whatever works for you and whatever you feel helps you in your healing journey, go for it. Be it once a year or seven times a year, there's no right or wrong way of healing, and there's certainly no time limit. Joy feels she's mourning that little girl who walked into that cabin. "I don't know who I would have been, who that little girl was. I have no memory of my life before my accident. I remember my grandpa dying and that's it. He died three or four months before my accident. I remember him dying and, yeah, I don't remember anything before my accident other than that."

Joy points out that resilient people aren't immune to stress and negative emotions. The stress and negative emotions will eventually seep into their lives, no matter how strong they try to be. If they don't address the issues, they will build up, and the person may eventually experience a breakdown. They can't live in denial and pretend everything is fine forever.

Taking care of one's self is vital, and Joy believes this is key to our mental health journey: "Mental illness doesn't just go away, even if you're medicated or seeing a therapist. I think it's the same as any illness, such as a cold or the flu. You've got to rest, and you've got to take care of yourself to be better. And if you don't, you just won't get better or it will take a lot longer to get better. I think that's the same with mental illness or even mental health. If you don't stay on top of it, you suffer for it. I actually didn't stay on top of it. I was diagnosed as clinically depressed when my oldest was just a baby, and I didn't feel okay in my head. Mother's Day last year, I had a complete breakdown. It scared me enough to go to the doctor the next day. I told him I didn't know what's going on. He diagnosed me with depression (again) and anxiety and put me on medication that, thankfully, is helping. What worried me though is that that was May 2017.

"I'm not big on New Year's resolutions, but in January 2017, I thought 'This is going to be my year; I'm going to live positively; I'm going to take care of myself.' Life was good! I was positive. Every day I was just trying to live a positive and good life, and then all of a sudden on Mother's Day, I was just…I think things were coming at me, and I was just like, 'Nope, not going to deal with it, not going to deal with it,' and I was letting things build up, and then on Mother's Day I had my breakdown."

But Joy is never one to take things lying down, and she now knows what tools she has to get through the hardest of times. If there's a lot going on Joy's life, and she doesn't deal with it, she knows that's not okay. But she also knows there's a light at the end of the tunnel. When she looks back at her life—not just at her accident—she knows she's struggled through those times, and that things get better and better in time. Don't give up, and don't be ashamed to ask for help. Nobody goes through hell forever. Stay positive, and remember everything is temporary.

Drawing from more recent experiences, Joy uses a variety of tools to get through her struggles. Joy had Gestational Diabetes when she was pregnant with Sahtaysha, so when Joy gave birth to her, Sahtaysha was having difficulties breathing properly on her own. The nurses immediately took Sahtaysha to the NICU (Neonatal Intensive Care Unit). Joy knew something was wrong because it wasn't like that with her first-born. She wanted to hold her baby right away. But it wasn't until four hours later that she was finally able to hold her. Sahtaysha spent only five days in the NICU, but it was a really long five days for Joy. She says she would rather experience her accident ten times over than feel what she went through when her youngest was born.

One tool Joy used was gratitude, gratitude, and more gratitude: "I kept reminding myself that it could be worse. There are a lot of other babies here that are really sick. She was one of the healthiest. I remember telling myself, 'I deserve her, and she's going to be ok.' I just tried to keep positive, even though I was crying all the time; I was a wreck. It was only five days, but it felt like five years. I just kept reminding myself that it would be okay. Today is hard, but it's easier than yesterday, and tomorrow is going to be easier too."

Joy has some important words of wisdom to share for anyone going through a rough time: "The first one is what my dad said to me. Even though I hated it so much at the time, I now have it tattooed on my ankle. He would always say, 'No pain, no gain.' I hated it because I thought, 'I'm in enough friggin' pain, come on.' He refused to baby me; he just wants to see me succeed. So he would always say, 'No pain, no gain.' Now I understand it. I think it fits no matter what anybody is going through, and it's my slogan for my "Scarred, Not Broken" webpages—just take it one breath at a time. Everybody says, 'Take it one day at a time,' but sometimes we're going through something so hard that we've just got to take it one breath at a time. Just breathe in and breathe out. Stay positive. Believe in the universe, and everything will work out how it's supposed to. Sometimes it's not how we want it to be—let's face it, people die, people get cancer, you know. These things happen. But there's a reason for everything. I truly believe that. And sometimes you don't find out what that is until years later. With me, for years, I cried to God 'Why, why did this happen to me?' And now I know why. I don't think it was planned, but I do think it's so I can help other people."

Love, Support, Compassion and Forgiveness

Elder and Knowledge Keeper Shirley Rabbit was born and raised in Maskwacis, Alberta. She currently lives in Montana First Nations, which is one of four bands that form Maskwacis. Even though she's 62 years old, she's not technically an Elder yet. Someone becomes an Elder either when they turn 65 or when their first grandchild is born. Although Shirley doesn't meet these criteria, her community acknowledges her as an Elder.

Over a year ago, the father of Shirley's children, David Matosk, took his own life. The suicide shook Shirley and her family to the core of their being: "We didn't see it coming," Shirley says. "Well, we did, yet we didn't. It just happened. Of course it shook us to our core. I'm prepared to talk about it because of the impact it had on each generation. My children's father committed suicide because he was born to and raised by parents who came from a residential school background.

"His mother, Annie Aldena Matosk, started sharing her story with us about five years into my relationship with David—what she went through and everything that happened, to a point. For myself, I watched his family and saw how it affected them."

Not only did David's parents go through the residential school system, but David also went through it himself for two traumatic years. "My dad also went through it for two years," Shirley explains. "So my family also suffered consequences from it. But you don't really live the trauma day-to-day. I could see the effects my dad's experience had on my family without fully understanding residential schools at the time, but I could see the effects on David's family even more. There was a lot of anger, a lot of unresolved issues. There were only three sisters and David. They had a difficult time having healthy communication with each other. Not long after David passed, the oldest sister died of a massive heart attack. He died in February, and his oldest sister died in June—right within the same time period. They got along to a point, but there wasn't any closeness between all of them that I could see. I used to wonder why, because there was just the four of them.

"It's very different in comparison to my family and how our mom (Mariah Rabbit) raised us. We're a big family; there are 12 of us. I come from a large family, and we were all born and raised with the teachings. That is, the teachings of love, support, compassion, and forgiveness. We live these beliefs in our daily lives, as compared to someone who went through the residential school. That's where I started to see the difference.

"I'm not saying our family didn't have our share of disagreements, just as any family. But just the two years my father was in the residential school affected him. And in turn, it affected us. But my mom balanced it out with her love. She's still alive; she's 90 years old. Still to this day, she's there wherever she's needed. That's what she taught us through the teachings as compared to my children's father, who received none of those teachings. When we started staying together, it was hard for him to understand things like forgiveness. He couldn't grasp things like that—to forgive, to walk in love. But he did manage to do it with our own kids. He helped me raise our kids in a healthy way. He was a good father to them.

"But he never had that teaching because after leaving the residential schools, people turned to alcohol and other addictions. Then there was the Sixties Scoop (whereby the government ordered the shutdown of residential schools and had Children's Services remove Indigenous children from their families and put them into homes in the United States and Europe. Many of these survivors are now going back to their communities to re-learn their culture). And they went through that too. They went through the abuse—physical, mental, sexual. That was the harsh background my children's father came from. We did end up separating because, even though I would encourage him and talk to him, there was so much more to it. It's difficult to help somebody so stuck in the past. But he was a good person.

"It was also generational," Shirley continues. "The anger, the unforgiveness, were passed down to his children. But to this day, I teach them love, compassion, goodness, getting along, understanding, patience … all the things my mom gave us. My oldest will be 32, and she just had her first child. My son is 27 and my youngest is 23. Overall, I have eight grandchildren from all my kids. I'm on my fifth great grandchild. I'm telling my oldest grandson that he's going to have a wife and children when he's 16 (kidding of course!) so we can have six or seven generations.

"My mom is 90, and she's still very alert and independent. Mind you, she was abused by my father. But she came from a protected, stable, and loving family. They used to give the young lady to the man. That's what happened to her. She was given away— an arranged marriage. She had no choice. She was only 14 when she was given for marriage. But she worked with it because she had a strong family background and strong faith. When alcohol became legal and was allowed in First Nations, my dad got caught up in it. A lot of these residential school survivors are still alive. They just didn't, and still don't, know how to deal with the pain.

"Part of this was because of our cultural practices, ceremonies, and beliefs being eroded and being outlawed and oppressed. We lost a lot of the ceremonies that were there to help people on their journeys. At the time residential schools started up, colonization affected First Nations across Canada. Our practices, our traditional beliefs, our ceremonies—a lot of them had to go underground. A lot were not practiced anymore because of what was happening. I'm lucky that my community stood firm in their beliefs and kept practicing. We welcomed the Christians, but we weren't affected by the Catholic school system even though it was the Catholic school system that ran the residential schools. Everybody has to understand that; there's a huge difference. Catholicism is a man-made religion. They made it to benefit themselves. For their own convenience. That's why they were able to do what they did. Their mandate was to kill the Indians and their children. The residential school system was supposed to civilize the savage, in part by getting rid of the language. That's what the Catholics did through the residential schools. A lot of the time these schools were very poor and didn't have much funding because all the money went to Vatican City. You've got to do a lot of research to see how all of these connect.

"To me," Shirley says, "resiliency was built into the teachings. Even David's mother had the teachings—that's why she's still alive today. She's going to be 80 years old. She went into the residential school when she was three years old, and she was there until she was 17. She was abused. She lost hearing in one ear, and now she's losing hearing in the other. Her kids blame her to this day for the abuse they went through. They haven't forgiven her. But she still goes on. She has her interests and whatever she needs to keep going. She's a very strong woman, though. After she went through residential school, she met and married David's father. He abused her, and he abused the children. All that stuff that came to be a part of a lot of First Nations' people's stories. I'm aware of some of this stuff—but this is our story, and it's about how we survived and can be sitting here now and talking about it. I'm talking because I want to share, because I want people to be aware.

"It was about finding a balance, a common ground to make things work. I didn't want my children to be affected by the past. It can have a lot of power, but we can also turn it around so our children can understand it. That's what I set out to do. Telling them stories, teaching them about what happened to their Kokum (grandmother) and what happened to their dad. Three women who personified and are symbolic of resiliency for me, and are still very much alive, are the grandmother (David's mother), my mother (Mariah Rabbit), and my aunt, who basically grew up with my mom because she was so young. This was my late dad's sister, Mary Rabbit. They all personify resiliency. I look up to them as my mentors. If they can do anything, I can do anything. Even Aunty Mary was abused because her husband went through residential school. They're not at a place yet to recognize how residential schools affected them. But I have had conversations with them, and I say, 'Hey, is it possible this is why it's happening?' But they're not open because they're younger than us. They're not really aware. Perhaps when they see their own kid's behaviours, they'll then be able to trace it back to residential schools.

"The mother was the balance. Anybody that went through residential schools, the Sixties Scoop, genocide, being put in a reserve like cattle—it all affects you. Then the Canadian government decided to destroy us even more by legalizing alcohol. This was about 1964 or 1965, and all hell broke loose. These were residential school survivors who suddenly had access to something that they could self-medicate with and numb the pain of all the horrors and abuse they went through in residential schools. The government is always one step ahead in ways they can destroy or do away the Indians. They don't realize they can't and are not going to. The Truth and Reconciliation was a laugh. It was their way, not our way. Still, some people in First Nations can turn it around and use it for themselves to build a positive and healthy community. It would be great. It's a start, but it's not a fix all.

"Our background goes back at least 500 years, and we're going to deal with that in, like, 10 years? It's not going to happen. But we can start teaching, and this is what I've done with my kids. We can start planting the seeds and educate and share our knowledge. We can say, 'Look, this is what happened, this is the past, and this is how it's affecting me. But you don't need the beginning part of it. It's done. You are different. You don't have to continue the cycle.'

"My children are dealing with their own addictions. But now they're fine. They've figured it out for themselves. We don't need to be there. Now they have to figure out who they are and what they want. That's how my mom talked to us and shared stories: We lived these teachings day-to-day. Now, in this day and age, they're going back to these teachings, and there are some misinterpretations and misunderstandings. 'This is how you do it,' and 'No, this is how you're supposed to do it.' It's kind of like a struggle in some areas. Now they're trying to make everything ceremony. But it's not. It's a way of life. You can't do ceremony for everything. It's a way of living the language and the beliefs."

Shirley's sister, Lavenia, also shares that what's missing in today's teachings is the emotional component, that is, how to be emotionally healthy. "A lot of them were not taught how to handle emotions," she says, "but I think it's basically what my mom grew up on. She was raised with love. She was happy to see her parents. My aunty was raised the same way. They were both raised on love. And I guess you can say that it's my mom's love for all of us that made us all close.

"My aunty and my mom didn't go to school," Lavenia adds. "They don't speak English."

Shirley says, in response, "At one point in time, I thought we should teach my mom. But something inside of me said, 'No, don't. Your mom is better off staying with that knowledge.' A couple of times she's said she regrets not learning. I tell her, 'Mom, no. It wasn't supposed to happen. You're fine, you're ok.'"

Lavenia continues, "My aunty also doesn't speak English. She and my mom just understand bits and pieces. And, in return, the grandkids are all learning our traditional language, so they have knowledge of our background."

Shirley adds, "Now the kids, when they have to communicate with her, have to try harder to learn and understand what she's saying. The ones that are older pick up the language. And the small ones too.

"Annie, the grandmother of my children, on their father's side, was very young. She had a loving background because her parents weren't in the residential school system. But she still went through abuse—mentally, physically and sexually. And then the bitterness and anger was passed on to her kids. She has three sisters and one brother, and they all went through the residential schools. That whole side of the family did. What happened was Annie's mother got sick and had to be kept at the tribe's council for three weeks. That's why her children were in a residential school. Back then, they were going to get you in one way or another.

"For some reason," Shirley says, "our little community of Montana First Nations held on and held their ground with the ceremonies and with the teachings. But that wasn't the case for the other First Nations, and I do see that difference. That's resiliency, because it's based on love, acceptance, and understanding. That's where I see resiliency coming from: forgiveness and letting go. My mom taught us that you're going to be the one carrying it if you don't forgive. So let go and move on. You can use it (resiliency) effectively and use it as a tool."

Shirley then changes the topic and takes us even further back in history. "Columbus never did discover America," she says. "It all started when he landed. He came from the Spanish Inquisition— that's the background he's from. When he landed in the Americas, death and destruction followed him. Death and destruction were already part of the Spanish Inquisition. How they idolized Columbus in the Americas and in the United States. Now, because First Nations are sharing their stories, he's being taken down and not looked up at as the hero they made him out to be because all he did was destroy the First Nations. And yet, despite all of that, the people still helped the Europeans. They never did conquer us. The Treaties were agreements; we never gave up the land. None. They were only allowed so much.

"Did you know," Shirley continues, "that there were hospitals just for Indians where Indians were experimented on? They brought over Chicken Pox and plagues with their blankets. Up until I was a child, they were still trying to kill us off. My mom still remembers the time we were given a box of tinned meat. She said it tasted really good, but after eating it, my siblings and I broke out in open sores. To this day, we don't know what it was. They destroyed the records.

"Those types of things, residential schools, the Sixties Scoop, the alcohol, and even our membership, were used against us. To be status, to be Metis, and the conditions put on that. You did this; we will starve you. You didn't behave; we will starve you. It's systemic genocide. Let's be real. It's not racism—racism is different. What we're experiencing is genocide—actual killings. All our missing and murdered women are a result of everything that's been happening for the past 500 years. This colonized thinking."

When David passed away, did family and friends help Shirley overcome this difficult time in her life? "They definitely helped," she says. "My immediate family, I mean. I don't have a whole lot of friends, just family."

I asked Shirley if she has a positive view of herself. "Well," she responds, "you should know body language. You tell me." I tell Shirley that I think she does, and that she comes across as a very confident person. "Well, there you go," she says. "I get that from my mother's teachings."

What about the ability to control her feelings and impulses? "It depends," she says. "If it's something scary, you react. The fight or flight response kicks in. But if it's something like drama, no."

Shirley seeks resources to help her when she's going through rough times. She was diagnosed with diabetes in 2007 and struggled with it for two years. After that, she knew she couldn't go back to work doing what she was doing. But then a foster parenting opportunity came her way and she took it. She believes in seeing what her options are, rather than seeing herself as a victim. She's proactive rather than reactive. Where there's a will, there's a way.

"So many times I've been at the bottom of the barrel," Shirley says, "but you learn different ways and techniques to get back up. There was a point in time when I started selling stuff, like a concession, at a ceremony called the Sundance—this was frowned upon, but I did it anyway. I did make a donation offer to the organizer. I did that for a number of years. You have to be creative and know what you can do and what you're capable of."

Does Shirley feel like she has control over her life? "Oh yeah," she says. "I'm where I need to be at. I've started the transition; I'm somewhere in the middle. That's where I'm at in being an Elder. Legally, you're not recognized as an Elder until you're 65. I'll be 63, so I'm almost there. My mom is still alive, so I feel she knows more than I do."

When something bad happens, Shirley sees herself as a strong person and sees this as an opportunity to help others. "Whether you see it as a negative or positive, it's a teaching lesson," she says. "You can take it as a blessing or a curse. It's up to you. But it's going to teach you something that's valuable to you. For me, I'll share what I believe."

What helps Shirley during tough times? "When I was able to, I was exercising and walking," she says. "When I can, I like walking around my place. Reading—I can read anything and everything. Give me something, and I'll read it. I can just Google or download books or look up books. It's opened a whole world for me. As a kid in Grade 4, I used to read the dictionary for the hell of it. I would finish the dictionary front to back." Shirley adds that ceremonies are also helpful for her.

I ask Shirley how her friends and family cope with stress. Shirley says that they are all there for each other, but they have different ways of coping. Shirley says she and Lavenia (her sister) are mostly together through stressful times. They mostly talk, text, or message each other. They also share quotes that bring a smile to their faces.

How important are negative emotions to Shirley, as a learning experience? "They're going to help you," she says. "You can choose to see them as a negative or positive; people will always label something anyway. But to me, it's all in one. There is no negative. It's all positive because it's going to teach you something of value."

In response to the idea that resilient people are immune to negative emotions, Shirley says she believes that that's very true. She believes that her resiliency maintains her health. Her two older sisters succumbed to diabetes—both of them had heart attacks and lost their limbs and had to do dialysis. "The trigger wasn't the diabetes; it was the loss of their loved ones," Shirley says, "and not dealing with it in a healthy way. The opportunities were there, but they didn't choose to follow the path of healing because they were so stuck in these areas. The key thing I see them struggling with is loss, broken hearts, heartaches. Loss of family is the big one.

"My oldest sister lost her baby, her son, through a tragic accident. My other sister died because she fell down the stairs. She wasn't diabetic; she died falling down the stairs because she was drinking. But she also had lost her son—her only son. And then my other sister, who also passed, lost the love of her life, her husband, when he died. My brother's wife died as well. And they couldn't handle it. I understand because I went through the same thing. But because of resiliency and being able to see through another day and learning how to help myself, I was able to move out and beyond it. I think, 'Wow! I went through that, and I'm still sitting here.' For me, it's because of the strong faith and belief our mother taught us, and me sharing this with my siblings too. My children's dad didn't have that, and that's so sad."

According to Shirley, perseverance and resiliency go hand in hand. You can't have one without the other. If you don't have perseverance, how can you have resiliency?

"It's ok to be frustrated," she says. "But don't follow that to the 't'. People are going to get frustrated regardless. You just get out of it and dust yourself off."

Humour is another tool or tactic Shirley uses to get through life's difficult moments. She also talks to friends and family. Shirley says she has a good support system, and she's there for others who are struggling. Both Shirley and Lavenia try their best to be there for others and to spread as much resiliency and perseverance as possible to help others get back to a healthy path.

What words of wisdom would Shirley like to share with someone who's struggling? "Suck it up butter cup! Just kidding!" she laughs. But then she becomes serious: "The first key is listening and letting them talk. And then finding common ground to start sharing. It may be a belief system that might help them, and then we can combine it with our ceremonial traditional beliefs, the Creator, and all that. I do a lot of serious talks and, like I say, I mostly just share what I know. For instance, I'll share an experience when I had something similar happen in my life. You connect with them. Of course it depends on the situation and what's going on because we're not all going through the same thing. Still, though, you connect, and you start building a foundation. But if I have just a few seconds or moments, I always use humour to lighten it up so it doesn't seem so harsh or permanent; it's all temporary. Encouraging them in the moment they're going through whatever they're going through is key."

Vivian of Arc

*T*hree years ago (2015), I opened up the autumn issue of my University of Alberta (U of A) Alumni magazine and read about a young lady who struggled with mental illness. When I finished reading her story, the first thing that came to my mind was, "Wow. This girl is brave." Brave not only in the sense of talking about her struggles so openly considering the stigma associated to mental illness, but also brave in the sense of talking about such a taboo topic AND being a Chinese person. I know what comes with the territory because I'm Chinese myself. I know what's acceptable, what's impressionable, and what can make you lose face. You just don't air your dirty laundry in public because you can lose face. But Vivian Kwan did it anyway, and I knew I wanted her story in my book. I saved the magazine and, three years later, I found her. Just like Joan of Arc who fought bravely and courageously in the battlefield, Vivian isn't fighting only an internal battle, but also a cultural one.

Vivian graduated from the U of A (University of Alberta) in 2015 with a Bachelor of Science with a major in biological sciences and a minor in psychology. While she was in school, she was fairly involved in non-profit and local grassroots organizations in Edmonton as well as other side projects. This was a great way to meet new people and to discuss new ideas. She recently started her Masters program in Public Health; working for the United Nations is her long-term goal. As well, Vivian also had the privilege of interning at the United Nations headquarters in New York City.

Vivian was born and raised in Edmonton, Alberta, Canada. Her parents were born in Hong Kong and China and immigrated to Canada. "They don't really understand the western culture and how they should raise their kids in terms of leaning towards the westernized culture or basing it on the more traditional Chinese culture," Vivian says. "Growing up, there was always that identity conflict for me, I guess. Do I identify myself as a local Canadian— going to school and learning English? Or do I hold onto the traditional Chinese values? I see how my parents were really conflicted with that, and it affected certain ways in which I think. I guess the most major thing that that kind of conflict planted in me in the last little while is the lack of conversations around mental health. Being the first child going to university was terrifying. My parents didn't go to post-secondary."

Vivian remembers her parents telling her that the most they could help her in school matters was at the junior high level. Vivian felt so overwhelmed with making decisions, finding available resources, and identifying whom she could talk to. And she had no role model either. Her parents couldn't help her navigate this new world that they themselves never took part in. Vivian really struggled for the first two years in university.

Depression and anxiety quickly set in for her, but she didn't know it. "I know now that depression and anxiety are basically imperative in my family, but none of us were diagnosed at the time," she says. "My grandma got diagnosed when she was 81. This kind of went on for a while—where you feel stressed, continuing stress, but you know it's not just stress. You can't figure out what it is. At the time, it was such a taboo to be one of those students who say, 'Oh, I'm going to go see a psychologist,' because if you tell your parents that, they'll be like, 'Oh, only crazy people go see psychologists.' Or they'll say, 'You're just stressed out. Once you sleep it off and exams are done, things will be ok.'"

Unfortunately, that wasn't the case. No matter how much Vivian wanted to believe what her parents were saying, she was feeling something else entirely. "So in third year," she says, "me and a long-term boyfriend at the time—we had dated for about three years—ended our relationship. It was a very, very rough breakup. There were just a lot of things happening in that winter semester in 2013. The breakup was really rough, and the moment when everything kind of fell apart was when he was drinking and driving because of the breakup. He got caught, and got a DUI because of that. I still remember that phone call: he called me at three or four in the morning. My friend didn't feel it was safe for me to go back home with him, so she kept me at her place. He would call me in the morning, already really drunk, and tell me that I had ruined his life because he got that DUI. I still remember that conversation. After that, a series of things just went crashing down. I had never felt the stress evolve to something so much more. At that point, I was like 'Oh my god—I don't think this is just stress.' I had no motivation to do anything. Classes were held literally five minutes away from where I was staying, but I just couldn't get to class and couldn't get myself together."

At the time, Vivian's friend was seeing a psychologist for her own personal issues, and she told Vivian it had been helping her. Her friend offered to go with Vivian if Vivian felt scared. Fortunately, Vivian went, with her friend by her side. When Vivian went to her appointment, she noticed a girl pacing back and forth in front of the clinic's front door. Vivian noticed the hesitancy and the anxiousness in the girl's eyes and could tell that she was debating whether she should go into the clinic or not.

Vivian walked up to her: "It was kind of weird because there was a mutual understanding of like 'Are you coming in to see a psychologist today too?' She said 'Yeah. It's my first time.' I said it was my first time too, and that we could go in together. I guess it was a very brief, short-term friendship that we established. Every now and then, I would see her at the Student Union Building, where the clinic is. Sometimes I would stop by and chat. She also introduced me to another of her friends. Both of them lived in Lister Hall (a student residence building). They would tell me things, and I got to know a little bit about their stories and told them a little bit about mine. That little supportive network formed over time in a period of about three to four months. But it was unfortunate, because it was very short-lived."

After awhile, Vivian didn't see them around anymore. When Vivian finally bumped into one of the girls, she realized something was very wrong: "The friend I met through the first girl told me that the first girl had committed suicide and passed away. It didn't hit me like reality, because she, well….why is someone just gone? They're just gone just like that. I think the worst part was that it created a kind of trigger effect. A week or so later, that friend passed also, also from suicide. It was just strange.

"I had the chance to meet their families. It was very mind-blowing for me at that time when I realized that their families didn't want their names to be publicized. Or, they would be like, 'This is such a shameful thing or a shameful way to die.' They didn't even want to make it public to raise awareness, and I was, like, 'Why?' The more traditional Chinese families would keep this under the rug. I have a lot of friends who were born and raised here but are from very traditional Chinese families. You don't see a lot of us talking about it openly. You know a lot of people have a lot of problems underneath, but nobody's willing to talk about it. Then it becomes a bigger problem."

That was an incredibly hard year for Vivian. She spiraled back and forth from suicidal thoughts to survivor's guilt. Vivian wondered why she made it through but her friends didn't. Was it because she didn't help them enough, or because she didn't notice something she should have noticed? Vivian blamed herself a lot. Eventually, she spoke about her thoughts and feelings with a friend, and that friend helped her through it: "They said to me, 'There's nothing you can do. Even if you noticed that there was something wrong, there's nothing you could do.' Beating yourself over something you can't control just makes it worse."

This inner turmoil and struggle lingered with Vivian for over a year. Then she received an official diagnosis of depression and anxiety. She started her anti-depressant medication, but noticed it didn't have an immediate effect. Even after a month, she didn't really notice a difference, and she still felt the same. Still, her doctor and pharmacists warned her not to stop taking the medication because it could mess up her brain chemicals, and she might feel even worse. Vivian didn't listen and stopped cold turkey for a year or two before getting back on it.

During the time she was off of it, she says, "It was disastrous. It was terrible. I sort of remember not feeling like me at all. It's like you're another person who you don't recognize. You're still you, but you're just in a body on autopilot going through the day. You have no emotions at all. It honestly took a long time before I realized there was something more I could do. I'm really lucky that the U of A has such a supportive network. It's kind of funny because, before I got to that extreme situation, I had been volunteering a lot. I met some people who worked at the University's Wellness Services, and most of them are public health professionals. So they coordinate most of the campaigns, and I had the opportunity to talk to one of them."

The person Vivian talked to noticed there was something going on with her. At the time, one of the center's initiatives was a mental health campaign. So this person brought up the suggestion of Vivian playing a role in this important project. That's when Vivian admitted what had been happening to her. "They were very supportive and understanding," she says, "and basically told me to look at it from a different perspective. They challenged me to channel whatever negative experience I had into something positive. By contributing to the campaign, I would make it more effective for other students. I started working on the project and continued until the end of my undergrad. I began to feel like I belonged again. I had felt so disconnected for so long because I basically isolated myself from everything. Being able to find purpose and to engage with the campus community again really helped because I was able to talk to people who understood, and that opened up the conversation for everybody there."

Vivian stresses that she didn't get completely better after her experience with the U of A Wellness Services, but it certainly helped her on the road toward better mental health.

I asked Vivian if her friends and family helped or hindered her emotional journey during this difficult time in her life. "Surprisingly," she says, "they actually really helped, but in a really interesting way. My friends have always been very open-minded in these kind of conversations. That was definitely a major thing that helped a lot in terms of opening up to my parents. I didn't actually realize this before. My parents never talked about mental health in the past. Not because they're against discussing it—it's just that they didn't really understand it when they were growing up. In their families, this was just not discussed. One evening, a year after my diagnosis, I finally talked to my parents about it. I thought about it, and was, like, 'I feel we should have this conversation.' I said to my mom, 'Remember back in the day you told me that the stress was something temporary? That once school is done, it'll be gone?' I told her honestly, 'I just saw a doctor, and I'm seeing a psychologist. It's not something temporary.'"

Vivian told her mom that she was officially diagnosed with depression and anxiety, and that she had been prescribed medication. This is huge for any parent to hear, but with Chinese families, it's massive. "I sort of remember her reaction," Vivian says. "She didn't really have much of a reaction. She was just, like, 'So, is this going to go away eventually?' I replied, 'It can get better, but it'll be with me for as long as I live.'"

Vivian tried to keep the conversation with her mom lighthearted, but that may have worked against Vivian because her mom didn't really sense how bad Vivian's struggles were. Vivian also had moved out of her parent's home during that dark period in her life, so her parents didn't see Vivian spiraling down first-hand. Her mom said, "You look so normal."

"People who look like me aren't always 100% well," Vivian stresses. "That's when they (her parents) had their first exposure to depression. I also suspect it runs in my family because my mom also has a lot of outbursts in very emotional times.

"She's hyper-sensitive to certain things. She'll just breakdown and cry out of nowhere. I don't really know why. I've said to her, 'Mom, have you ever thought about seeing someone? Because I feel this is something more that may run in the family. I see the similarities in me, you, grandma. I feel like this is something more.'"

Vivian's mom, who is currently 54, didn't think it was a priority. She said she could function normally on a daily basis and could go to work. "It's just a bunch of excuses," Vivian says, "She's coming up with reasons to say, 'No, I don't want to go.'" For the most part, Vivian is very thankful her family has been pretty supportive. There wasn't any denial on their part, and they've tried to understand what Vivian was and is going through. But there were times when her family would make comments clearly showing they haven't fully comprehended the magnitude of Vivian's struggles. It's not easy for any parents to hear about their children's struggles with mental illness, but Vivian's are trying.

"My dad actually got diagnosed recently," Vivian says. "It's been an interesting switch in positions. I never imagined my dad coming to me and asking me about my experiences with antidepressants. He asks lots of questions: 'So, what dosage were you at?' 'How did it work for you?' He's just basically asking for feedback of how the process goes." Vivian feels really good and appreciative about her dad being so open with her about this. But her dad is still trying to adjust with the medication and determining which doctor works best for him. There was a point when he stopped taking the antidepressants, but that didn't help. The most important thing is that he's exploring what works for him and what doesn't, and he's being proactive and making an effort to get better.

Self-confidence comes and goes for Vivian, but, for the most part, it has been a struggle for her. "One thing I really learned a lot about in the last couple of years of my undergrad," Vivian says, "was the whole idea of Imposter Syndrome. Basically, the idea is that no matter how much you accomplish, you'll always feel like you're just an imposter, and you don't deserve your accomplishments. I remember really clearly talking to one of my exes about it. I don't know what it is, but I can't seem to say or name one thing that I'm very proud of that I've done in my life. I'm constantly unsatisfied, searching for that one thing without knowing what it is. With the whole UN (United Nations) internship thing, everyone is like, 'Wow! That's such an accomplishment! That's such a big thing for you!' But for me it just feels like another trip. Is it because I'm really capable of doing it, and that's why I got selected for it? But then I can't help but feel self-doubt … I tell myself I just made it because I'm lucky. You'll always say that it's because you're lucky and not because of your ability. And there are so many times, regardless of what life events come out, like winning an election, because I'm very lucky, not because I put in the hard work. It just goes on and on and on. Sometimes when I do things that I know I'm very good at or I can see the results right in front of me, I'm more confident because I see results. But for things that are up in the air, there's no metric to measure success. That's when I kind of go back and forth a little bit. Am I actually doing a good job, or am I actually just cruising by? And that's when the whole question of self-esteem comes in."

Growing up in a traditional Chinese family didn't make things easier for Vivian. "Even if you get 99% on an exam, where's that missing 1%? So, you'll always ask yourself that … people say I'm doing pretty well, but what about the things I didn't, or don't, do well? You'll always think about the things you could have done better on." This running dialogue in Vivian's mind has shaped her thoughts about success along with her self-esteem and self-confidence. Vivian comes across as a very articulate and confident young woman. But she sometimes feel people don't know what's going on inside of her.

Vivian considers herself a logical person. "I think for me," she says, "I'm logical because I'm scared of acting on my feelings; I don't like the sense of not being in control. So the whole situation of going through the whole depressive cycle and not being able to understand why I'm feeling a certain way is hard because I really like to analyze: 'Oh, I'm feeling upset because this and this happened.' It's always a very clear understanding of the series of events that contributed to how I feel. So not being able to control how I feel really scares me. For the most part, I'm not really impulsive. I really think things through before I act a certain way, I guess. I would never act based on how I feel. So in a way, that becomes very draining on a day-to-day basis because I really analyze every one of my actions."

Like a lot of people, Vivian's response to tough times is to internalize her thoughts and feelings in order to cope. It may work temporarily, but not for long, she says: "When you internalize anything, it actually makes the situation worse. I chose to speak out. And what I found most effective is to talk about it. Even though we all know a lot of people who don't like to talk about certain topics, we tend to really underestimate the power of just a brief conversation. For me, the first time I was honest and open with a friend I really trusted about my situation, I was just so surprised to find how helpful it was to talk to somebody about it. Maybe they're going through something similar that you don't know about. And knowing that you're willing to share something so personal kind of sends them that cue that they can be comfortable sharing what they've been keeping hidden away. That's the power of dialogue."

There are tons of resources out there to help, but not a lot of people use them. Still, they're there for a reason. Maybe people don't use them just because they don't have the same power as a dialogue with someone else who may be going through the same things. Or perhaps the never-ending stigma behind mental illness and mental health holds people back from seeking professional help.

Vivian now feels she has a certain amount of control in her life. "Back when I was younger, when I was 18 or 19," she says, "I wouldn't say I felt like I had a lot. But there were also self-induced consequences where I chose to make bad decisions. I kind of just lived through the consequences of those bad choices. But now, for the most part, I think it depends on looking at what's important as opposed to what you can control. Let's say I'm making a steady income, and I'm doing what I want and doing what I enjoy. In that aspect, I have full control of how I choose to live my life. But in other events, I'm like, 'Oh, what if I get laid off from work?' In other situations where I have no control, I try to think, 'Well, that's that.' But, yeah, for the most part, when it comes to things that dictate my life or things that contribute to my standard of living, I think I have full control of my life."

Does Vivian see herself as a victim when something bad unexpectedly happens? "It's always hard not to dwell on a bad situation when something happens," she says. "So it's almost inevitable that the victimization feeling comes out now and then. I've seen people who just go in circles. Whenever something big or small that's bad—well, basically, anything they perceived as negative—they just go in circles. They can't get out of it. They always say, 'Why is this happening to me? This shouldn't be happening to me.' It goes on forever. It's not productive at all. I guess witnessing how certain people deal with it has taught me that this is not the way I want to handle things because I honestly see time as something that goes by really fast. I don't have time to go in circles and waste my time! Usually, I sort it out in my head, and ask questions: 'This thing that happened; was it bound to happen? Or was it something I couldn't control?' If it's something that, regardless of what you did, you couldn't have done anything differently, and it still would have happened, then I'll be, like, 'Okay, I didn't have any control, so all I can do is just accept the fact that it happened and move on.

"But if it's something like an action that I took that caused it to happen, I'll reflect on what I did prior to it happening and see how I can change it. That's the only way I can move on. Honestly, life's too short to just pause and think about things you can't control and be upset. I don't have time to do that! I don't even know what's going to happen tomorrow!" Does anybody really know?

Whenever Vivian has the opportunity to share her experiences, she sees it as both a blessing and a curse. During the terrible and difficult times in her life, Vivian learned some awful things, and she had to figure a lot of things out on her own. Still, she feels extremely lucky that she got through it on her own, and she sees it as a life lesson. It changed her perspective on many things. She gained valuable experiences that she wouldn't have gained if the terrible events never happened. She's now in a position to help others navigate the same situations she found herself in. "I see it as a particular advantage for me," she says, "being a woman of colour and also somebody from a Chinese background, where they don't talk about mental health. They see me, or hear me, and maybe think, 'This girl is talking about this. So why do I have to hide it away?' And that's the kind of movement I've been seeing whenever I talk to individuals. It's kind of interesting; when I was in Shanghai in November, I did a little project there about mental health. I talked to a bunch of different people from different age groups—students, professionals, expats, etc. We just talked about their mental health stories. We were at a press conference (in Shanghai), and I did my introduction first. I was the only Chinese participant there, which was interesting. I said that I have depression, I have anxiety, and I've lost friends to suicide. You could immediately see the reactions on the reporters' faces. They were older, more mature Chinese individuals. And they said, 'But you look so normal!'"

Wow! That's a very interesting, naïve, and ignorant observation on the reporters' part. Is there a certain look for someone with mental illness? Could it be that dishevelled, greasy-haired person shuffling through a back alley looking through garbage? Or could it be that person you call father, co-worker, or best friend? Unless you're a mind reader, nobody really knows what's going on in another person's mind. They could be presenting themselves as very happy-go-lucky to their friends, family, or the public, yet they can be struggling internally. Mental illness is indiscriminate of any background. We have to be careful about jumping to conclusions about people.

I asked Vivian how she copes during tough times and when she's stressed. Healthy or not, Vivian likes to get involved in as many different projects as possible. She takes on a lot of things. If she's not working, she's volunteering. If she's not volunteering, she's doing school work or other things. But Vivian does keep track of how much she's taking on and is conscious of what's too much and what she's comfortable with. She gets a sense of fulfillment from the time she spends volunteering, whether with grassroots organizations that focus on addictions or supporting mental health for youth. "I find the three hours I spend with them (the youth) so rewarding that I don't see it as a commitment, or volunteer work. I sort of remember back in the days when I was working with the SU (Students' Union) doing similar work. I worked 80 hours a week, but I wouldn't feel tired at all. I guess I cope through work, but I don't see it as work. I find it really hard to explain it to my friends—'No no no. It's not work. It's almost like a hobby.' I'm just doing a lot of this hobby." The work and volunteering are therapeutic for Vivian, and it works for her, and that's what matters at the end of the day, regardless of what anybody else thinks. Knowing that she's making a difference in other people's lives and that she's helping others makes Vivian happy. She enjoys talking to people, sharing stories, and learning new things. Through these experiences, she gains new perspectives she's never known before, and they inspire her.

Do her family and friends cope with stress in a similar way? Vivian says her parents internalize everything, which she doesn't think is healthy. She also notices the same for some of her friends who aren't really open with their emotions. She can tell they're stressed out. She sees these resemblances between her parents and friends when she talks to them. Some people who she knows are struggling adopt unhealthy ways of coping. For example, they spend a lot of money as they shop, shop, and shop. They're stressed out about money in the first place, but try to ease this anxiety by spending money to go shopping. More often than not, guilt overcomes them when the credit card statement arrives. It's a vicious cycle that may never end.

Understanding her negative emotions and struggles and how it can be a learning experience is important to Vivian. "Honestly, you can't be happy 100% of the time. Every now and then I'll still have negative emotions like disappointment, or I'll think 'Why did I do that?' It loops around in circles. It's so important to recognize that emotion. I tell people I talk with that every sense of emotion you're feeling is valid. You shouldn't try to explain why you shouldn't feel that way, delegitimize it, or tell yourself it's not how you should feel. Just own up and try to understand why you feel the way you do. A lot of times I'll hit a bump and feel upset for whatever reason on that day. Once I get the time to sit down by myself, or talk to somebody, and try to understand why I'm feeling that particular way, it really helps me learn more about myself; a lot of people would choose to avoid negative feelings. Sometimes people will blame certain events or blame other people. But you never really think about yourself … how do you, yourself, tie into this negative emotion?"

Vivian isn't a confrontational person, so when a friend pointed out to Vivian how Vivian had hurt them, without Vivian even realizing it, Vivian owned up to it. She apologized for her actions, and she reflected on the situation. She knew she couldn't turn back time, but she could acknowledge the situation and become more cognizant of and sensitive to what she says moving forward. As hard as it was, this was the best plan to move ahead for both parties. It was both a lesson and a growing experience for Vivian in her quest to become a better person.

What are Vivian's thoughts on resilient people being immune to stress? She feels it's true to a certain extent. Sure, there will be times when you know how to handle a situation, but then there are the curve balls of life: "Oh, this is a whole new level of stress I don't know how to deal with, I sometimes think," she says. "But because you went through so many tough situations in the past, you kind of have a feel of what to expect. I think it helps for the most part. I guess even talking about understanding your negative emotions and understanding how your body reacts to stress really helps you decipher a little bit of what that new stressor might be." The negative emotions help people navigate through life a little bit better, and it takes less time to figure things out when the next curve ball comes. Vivian understands there's going to be curve balls flying at her left, right, and center. Though she may not react perfectly, she knows how to handle it for the most part. She has a general framework for how she will handle certain situations.

In Vivian's view, the relevance of the term *perseverance* in the mental health world depends on the context. "Ultimately, if I were to look at the term *perseverance* for my situation, or, let's say, for someone who has a goal in mind of getting well and wanting to do something more, then of course there's a purpose to persevering through the tough times. But when I think about the people who don't see that goal, especially people like my friends who obviously didn't see the purpose of living and took their own lives, how does the term *perseverance* apply to them?

"As you talk to individuals who struggle with mental health about perseverance, it's very hard because everybody's context is different. It depends on what you mean by persevering. Do you mean persevering through the difficult time and then you're fine again? It kind of depends on how they interpret it too. If you're talking to someone who clearly doesn't have the will to live anymore, perseverance doesn't mean anything to them."

One of Vivian's favorite quotations is this: "Do one thing every day that scares you!" Vivian used to be petrified of public speaking. "I told myself, 'Oh, you have to do it. The only way you're going to get better is if you go out there and go against your fear and actually do it.'" Embrace your negative emotions. There's always going to be good and bad stress that can push someone to grow and understand themselves a bit more. For Vivian, she acknowledges the particular stressor and uses it for something good.

I asked Vivian about any other tools or thought processes she uses to help her through difficult times: "At times, it gets really, really difficult. It's still manageable, but I still get frustrated and mad, but all of the negative emotions are under control. Usually when I get really mad—that does happen—for the most part, I read a lot of non-fiction books. Anything empowering that talks about women in leadership. I really like historical analysis as well. Sometimes I'll randomly find a good fiction that's still based on real events. I guess it's interesting because sometimes my mind will be really invested in something negative that's happening, and I can't think it through. Reading a different book opens up my mind to a different perspective and to a whole different topic, so that kind of distracts for a little bit. But I'm also able to learn something new in a different way. I quite enjoy that. It's just so much harder when I'm working full time and I'm tired all the time; in that case, it's harder to pick up a book without falling asleep."

Vivian also tried listening to podcasts, but couldn't really get into it. A lot of her friends are into it, but Vivian finds it doesn't work for her. It's a personal preference, and it's not for everybody. Volunteering, talking to others, reading — what other tools does Vivian use to get through difficult times? "Some days I don't feel very social," she says. "Sometimes I'll shut myself down for three days just to get some 'me' time. Maybe I'll sleep a lot or I'll watch a lot of television until it gets to the point where I need to see another person because I don't know how to speak anymore. That would be an option. I still exercise four times a week, but not because of stress. I just incorporate it into my lifestyle. I feel okay or better after doing it, but I don't necessarily go just when I'm stressed. I try to do it like a daily thing. That kind of helps boost my mood. I used to shop a lot, but I realize the potential damage, especially while going back to school, so that's a no-no."

What would Vivian say to people going through a rough time in their lives right now? "All your feelings are valid, good or bad," she says. "It's okay to feel negative emotions because sometimes those are the emotions you'll learn from. The biggest push is for you to learn something more about yourself. Don't be afraid to start a conversation; once you take that first step—which is usually the hardest step—to talk about something so personal, you're opening doors to places where other people are privately struggling. Sometimes they just need that one person to start that ripple effect. Someone to say, 'Hey, you're not alone.' That's what I notice. I felt alone for so long. Everybody around me seemed to be living such a good life. They were healthy; they weren't experiencing anything negative like I was. And I'm afraid to be a downer by bringing up negative feelings. So I choose not to. But once I began delivering it in the proper way, the feedback I received was so positive. It turned out that people who I thought had perfect lives struggled as well. That's when you realize you're never alone. Mental health issues touch everybody, regardless of how severe—it could even be something as simple as stress about an exam. Every type of feeling of stress is valid. If people need to talk about it, they should talk about it."

Brotherly Love

Born in Edmonton, Alberta in 1954, Wei Wong spent his early formative years in the Calder area. The Wong's first home was on the northwest corner of the family's market garden. For those familiar with Edmonton, the 20-acre market garden sat north of the train tracks on 127 Avenue and 113 Street. A few years later, Wei and his family also gardened at the Beverly farm, which was also 20 acres. To get there, you take 118 Avenue across to Edmonton's River Valley and turn right at the guardrail, where there's a plot of land on the east side of the bridge on the river flats.

Wei's parents ran their own market garden business with Wei's father working as the gardener. Wei's father, Bark Ging Wong, and mother, Young See Wong, were both born in Guangdong Province in China, in the district of Toishan. Bark Ging Wong came to Canada with no education in 1921, when he was 13 years old.

"In 1923," Wei explains, "the Chinese Exclusion Act was passed by the Canadian government, virtually banning all immigration from China. My father would have been 15 years old at the time, and wouldn't have known when or if he would ever see his family again. Despite his situation, he was expected to find work to support himself and to send remittances home to support his family—father, mother, brothers, and sisters. He found employment as a labourer, cook, and market gardener. In 1930, he travelled back to his ancestral village in China to get married. He came back to Canada alone, not knowing when he might see his bride again. In 1947, the Chinese Exclusion Act was repealed, and my mother was reunited with my father in 1949, 18 years after they were married. They were finally together and could start their own family in Edmonton. She was 37 at the time. Unbeknownst to me until I was an adult, my mother gave birth to a daughter in 1950, but the baby survived only a little over a month. My parents never spoke about this daughter as I was growing up.

"A little over a year later, a baby boy, Wayne, arrived in October of 1952," Wei continues. "Fourteen months later, I was born. I would remain the youngest in our family. My brother Wayne and I were very close. Our early years were spent on the family market garden in north Edmonton, where our home was located. As soon as we could walk, we learned to do chores to help the family business. As a family, we kept to ourselves because our home was on the 'wrong side of the tracks' if you will. My first home was in Calder, on land north of the Canadian National rail yards along 127th Avenue. We had no plumbing and no running water. My father, having experienced the consequences of the racist laws of the Canadian government, kept our family close. My parents managed to befriend a few non-Chinese neighbours who became long-term friends. We grew up in a sheltered atmosphere away from Chinatown, where most of my father's trusted compatriots lived and worked. We moved to a new home in Dovercourt in 1958. In 1959, after winding up our market gardens in Calder and Beverly, a new parcel of land was purchased further north to start a new market gardening venture. We spoke mostly Toisanese at home before starting public school.

Wayne and Wei, Calder area, 1956

"After Wayne's first day in public school, the administration told my parents that his English wasn't good enough and advised them to register him for the following year. As we got to know our neighbourhood better in Dovercourt, we made friends with a few other children. I think I had an easier time learning English as we settled in. I was a quick study, following Wayne's example. Wayne started back to school, and I followed the year after. We both joined Cubs at the urging of a neighbour, and we enjoyed the activities in the basement of Kirk United Church once a week. We participated in the Boy Scout camp at Skelton Lake. Wayne was a good student in school, and I was eager to learn as well. My marks were very good at the time. The public school practice back then was to accelerate exemplary students, meaning that the school let me skip Grade 3, so I ended up in Grade 4 with my brother. If we were close before, in a relative sense, we were even closer now.

"It felt great to be in the same grade as my brother. I was proud to be there with him. We competed to see who could get the highest marks. As a younger brother, of course, I bugged him about all manner of things. If I didn't understand something, Wayne was my go-to guy. I also hung around with his friends. We invariably walked to and from elementary school along with another friend who lived nearby. But Wayne and I weren't always in the same class, which gave him a break from me. In junior high, we didn't have any classes together. He was more skilled in making things in Industrial Arts class and was more confident using tools. He made more friends in junior high, whereas I mostly stuck with the friends I had met in elementary school. Wayne was an honours student in both junior high and senior high, and I wasn't far behind. For both of us, math was our favourite subject. Together, we completed high school in 1971. For all the years we were in school, we spent spring weekends, summer vacation, and fall weekends helping on the farm. We transplanted seedlings, weeded row upon row of vegetables, repaired crates, filled orders, harvested vegetables, washed and packed vegetables, and helped with deliveries.

"After graduation from high school, we still helped my parents in the market gardening business, but we also looked for jobs to help pay for our university tuition. Wayne took the lead and was the first to secure a job at a sod farm. I enquired after he did and got a job there too. These jobs involved physical labour, but we were used to it. The hours were long, but we were pleased to be able to pay for our post-secondary education on our own. Both of us started at the University of Alberta in the Faculty of Science. Wayne directed his focus to Computing Sciences while I continued with Mathematics. The next summer, we once again worked for the same employer. The employer noticed Wayne's initiative and leadership skills. He was fast at adapting to any job, quick to learn the operation of new machinery, and good at motivating others to do their jobs well.

"The third summer we worked there, the company wanted to establish a tree nursery, and Wayne was given a leadership role and became the supervisor. Before summer was out, he was offered the position of Nursery Manager. He embarked on taking courses in soil sciences and pesticide application and decided not to continue as a full-time student at university. He took on more responsibilities and made trips to different tree nurseries to research their operations and source stock. I obtained a Bachelor of Science with Honours in Mathematical Statistics in the spring of 1975. With paper in hand, I started looking for a different job. Our family market gardening business wound up at the end of that year, and the property was sold in 1976. My parents started their well-deserved and long-awaited retirement. Wayne seemed to enjoy the challenges of establishing the tree nursery and advanced to managing several people in the operation. I accepted a new opportunity and left Edmonton in September of 1975 to train in Ottawa. My brother continued to work and live at home with my parents.

"After completing my training in Ottawa with the Federal Department of Transport in 1976, I was posted north of the Arctic Circle in Inuvik, then shortly after was transferred to Tuktoyaktuk on the Arctic Ocean. I spent a winter there, a place where you didn't see the sun rise for a few long weeks in winter, and where you had a period of 24 hours of daylight in the summer. After my stints there, I was transferred to High Level, Alberta. I regularly corresponded with my brother; we compared jobs and weather, and I inquired about our friends and our parents. On special occasions, I would phone home to keep in touch. The winter months were always a slow time after working hard at the market garden, and it was the same for the tree nursery operations.

"At one point, my brother planned a trip to see me in High Level. I had described to him my sparse living conditions, the potentially hazardous road conditions, and the lack of entertainment many times in my letters to him. Besides that, I was scheduled to work when he planned to visit. Also, Edmonton was already cold enough. I couldn't figure out why anyone would want to travel even further north in the winter. Nevertheless, he showed up. For a week, we spent some time together cross-country skiing and visiting my friends. It was good to see him, but I was still perplexed as to why he didn't take a vacation to a warmer destination. After he left, it was back to routine for the next several months through spring and the start of summer.

"But that fateful day on June 16, 1978, I received a shocking phone call at work that shook me to the core. I was told that my brother had died. I couldn't believe it. For a few moments, which seemed like an eternity, my mind stopped, my breathing ceased. I was in a fog—completely overwhelmed. Then I was told that he died by suicide in the basement of my parents' home. I felt sick to my stomach. I was devastated. I couldn't comprehend what had happened. I was pulled off my work position. I was numb as I went home to pack. I flopped down on my bed and cried: 'Why, why, why?' The agent for the airline put me on the only flight out on compassionate grounds."

After Wayne's passing, Wei and Wayne's family and friends came together to support Wei during that tragic time. For Wei's parents, as for any parents who have lost their child, the pain they carried was an unbearable grief they never talked about.

"My brother was only 24 when he died," Wei says. "Most of his friends were those he made in school. They all lived close by and knew each other. They came together or alone to offer condolences. Two of them are still my lifelong friends. For most of them, my brother's funeral was the first one they had ever attended. They stepped up as pallbearers, so that helped immensely. It was a comfort to have them around. It was a difficult time for everyone all around. It was a family friend who had delivered the bad news to me while I was in High Level. He and his wife had been fast friends with our family since Wayne and I were toddlers. They socialized often with my parents, and were true friends to the end of their days.

"By this point, my family had lived in the same house for 16 years. As things settled down, my parents realized they couldn't bear to live in the house where this tragedy happened. They moved out of the neighbourhood three months later. It still pains me to know that my parents had to go through this after all the adversity they had already endured. No parent should have to lose a child. To bury two children was an immense burden to bear for the rest of their lives. Besides that, suicide carries a stigma for many, and my parents were no different. They didn't talk about it, taking their own thoughts to their graves."

Wei feels he is generally an optimistic person who tries to see the bright side of most things in life and the good in people. He feels most confident when he encounters situations he has control over or in situations he understands or has the training for, such as getting good grades at school or accomplishing another year at work. But when Wei finds himself in a new or unfamiliar situation, he feels he needs to build up his confidence. More often than not, he likes to be prepared; but how can anyone be prepared for the death of a sibling?

For the most part, Wei says he feels he has control over his feelings, but he likes to analyze what's in front of him before taking the next step. But sometimes life hands you a deck of cards you have no idea how to deal with.

"For the most part," Wei says, "I think I can control my feelings. I like to think things through before acting. In the days after his death, representatives from my brother's company came to the house to offer their condolences. I told my parents that they were waiting outside, but my parents refused to see them. In fact, they asked me to tell them they weren't welcome at the funeral. On the spot, I had conflicting feelings about that, but my parents were adamant. They believed that something had happened at work to trigger Wayne's actions. My guess is that his office called to inquire where he was that morning because it was out of character for him to be late. Not having seen Wayne, my father would have told them that he'd gone to work. I learned that, after receiving a second call from Wayne's work, my mother had gone downstairs and found the tragic scene. I will spare the details. I had no idea why my parents acted this way toward the representatives. But it wasn't the time to argue. I felt guilty as I communicated my parents' wishes to them.

"Wayne's death was never far from my mind," Wei continues. "Years later, I learned that a medical report that had been written four months before his suicide suggested that he had been over-exposed to organophosphate pesticides. It may not have been conclusive that it contributed to his troubled mind, but as a licensed pesticide applicator, his work exposed him to dangerous chemicals that could have affected his health. My parents' intuition may have been correct. They believed something at work had precipitated Wayne's death. I could no longer fault them for not welcoming his employer's representatives into our home.

"When my brother was alive, I think it was natural for me to get his opinion on pretty well everything. So when a problem came up, I would quickly share it with him. He was my mentor in many ways. It was a relief to have someone else working on my problems with me, but it may have turned out that I had given him extra burdens to carry. Since his death, I've had no choice but to try to solve problems on my own; I mainly keep my feelings to myself. I don't usually share my burdens with others."

I asked Wei if he feels he has control of his life. "We all have our insecurities," he answers, "but I feel in control of my life for the greater part. After Wayne's death, I had some serious doubts about whether anyone can have complete control of one's life. Quietly, I set some personal goals and timelines for myself, and I was proud of myself when I actually achieved them. My confidence returned gradually."

For Wei, his internal struggles and grief for Wayne's passing will always be there. But, as beyond heartbreaking as it was, something positive did transpire from this tragic event: Wayne's kidneys were donated to someone in need of a transplant, and he continues his legacy by having helped someone else live.

How does Wei currently get through difficult moments in his life? "If I keep busy," Wei says, "it limits my time to think about the rough times. Keeping the daily routine intact helps, and opting to help family members or delving into volunteer work gets me through the situation. Something as simple as washing the dishes, vacuuming the house, mowing the lawn, or getting together with family members helps me to stay grounded and centered. These activities redirect the negative energy from the situation to something positive.

"Most of my friends and family are well-adjusted," Wei says. "They're able to step back, look at a situation, and talk things through with family or friends to reason things out. As the saying goes, 'Two heads are better than one.' They usually already have it figured out before asking for another opinion, sometimes just for reassurance.

"I think negative emotions are important while making sure they're in check and don't take over your life. Overcoming each emotional struggle is a learning experience. I realized that my brother made a conscious decision in his state of mind to take his own life. And as sad as it was for all concerned, that was his will. But I can't dwell on how bad I feel forever because that would be utterly self-centered.

"What we can take away from this is how we can help others overcome a similar situation because, as much as this was a stark and unwanted learning experience, it was a learning experience all the same. Spiritual growth to me means that I have grown mentally by developing a broader awareness of the fragility of others. Maybe I have a greater capacity for forgiveness for someone like my brother, whose actions affected so many people. It wasn't his intention to harm anyone else, but his actions impacted their lives in so many ways. I can't even speculate what life might have been like for him had he lived. Would he have been disabled? Would he have married? Had children of his own? Things we will never know. At the time and in his frame of mind, he couldn't see a future for himself."

When it comes to the idea that resilient people are immune to stress and negative emotions, Wei says, "I can't accept the inference that resilient people are immune to stress and negative emotions. Resilient people might be able to conceal their stress or negative emotions better, but that may be detrimental to their mental well-being. Confiding in someone you trust can relieve a whole lot of stress. Sharing a burden is lessening a burden. Knowing that someone else understands your feelings means you are not alone."

For Wei, *perseverance* means being able to adapt to the changing environment or situation. Having a healthy balance in our life is vital, he says. This may look different for each person, but, as difficult as it is, leading a healthy life also means moving on. Moving on doesn't mean forgetting your loved ones or forgetting what's happened. Moving on means that you'll never forget them, but, at the same time, you need to move forward in life. Your loved ones would have wanted that. Continuously reliving what happened can be dangerous—it can become your 'new normal,' where you are simply existing rather than living.

"There are a lot of distractions in our daily lives," Wei says, "but if we persevere in our endeavours, we can reach a successful outcome. If you have a goal in mind, keep aiming for it. You may have to pace yourself, but keep going forward and don't give up. If we're limited by physical or mental abilities, we may be able to reach a reasonable compromise in attaining our goals."

Practicing empathy and understanding that there are a lot of other people in worse situations also helps Wei when he's going through difficult times: "If I think that my present situation is bad, I remind myself that there is always someone going through a situation that's a lot worse. We need to keep believing that there are better days ahead. These two words, *resilience* and *perseverance*, are attributes that truly exemplify my parents. They endured the pain of being separated from loved ones and the fear of an uncertain future at an early age. They experienced heartache and heartbreak multiple times. I can only imagine what they must have gone through. It must have taken years off their lives. All of my difficult times pale in comparison to theirs.

"Forty years have passed since my brother's death," Wei says. "The following sayings may be cliché, but the more I mature, the more sense they make: 'This too shall pass'—that is, whatever the situation, its impact will be felt less and less as time passes. 'Stop worrying about things you can't change, and do something about what you can change.' This is important to making your situation better, but it may require a major mental shift in thinking. 'We can't predict the future—so just make the best of it.' Your circumstances could actually be much better than you think!

"When I observe my five grandchildren interacting," Wei concludes, "it reminds me of how much fun it was growing up—free of worries and responsibilities. Every time I visit Wayne's grave, I can only imagine how life might have been had he stayed with us."

TRANSformation

Photography by: Aaron Pedersen.

Born into a prominent family that includes a long line of political leaders, knowledge keepers, medicine men, and activists from the Montana First Nations, it was only natural that Chevi Ray Lee Rabbit would be a leader herself, proudly beating her own drum while standing up for herself and for others. This young, bright, vocal leader was born and raised in Ponoka, Alberta and in Montana First Nations. Montana First Nations is one of the four bands that fall under the Four Nations of Maskwacis.

As an adult, Chevi began to ask questions about her father's family history. Tragically, Chevi's father, Calvin Currie, was murdered when Chevi was a child. Chevi's grandmother and grandfather, Jean and Frank Smith, both passed away in Vancouver, British Columbia before she had a chance to get to know them. Chevi's uncle, Frankie Currie, was taken during Canada's Sixties Scoop and has been missing for over 40 years, leaving a large monetary estate unclaimed. Chevi also learned that her aunt, Marlene Currie, was among Canada's missing and murdered Indigenous women in Montreal. As tragic as these circumstances are, the Currie family has done great things for First Nation communities; many of the family's members are academics involved in politics and community development.

Growing up, Chevi was (and still is) surrounded by a loving and supportive blended family that includes Chevi, her mom, her stepfather, and three step-siblings. Tragically, one of her step-siblings was killed in a car accident not too long ago. Chevi's mom and her stepfather have been married for 30 years, and Chevi's close relationship with the entire family has always made her feel she is part of a family rather than a stepfamily.

Important individuals Chevi admired as a child include her uncle, Chief Leo Cattleman; her aunt, Velma Cattleman; her late aunt, Cree Councillor Rema Rabbit; and her aunt, Shirley Rabbit, who is currently a respected Cree Elder in Maskwacis, Alberta. Although she never met her grandfather, Joe Rabbit, who was a farmer and Cree leader, she nevertheless has always been interested in hearing stories about him. Chevi also admires her late step-grandma, Sarah Schug, who was an Elder for Alberta's Central Child and Family Services. She also adores her grandma, Mariah Rabbit, who is well known for her knowledge of Cree culture and wisdom. Mariah was awarded an honourary doctorate by the Maskwacis Cultural College for her contributions to Plains Cree culture. It's obvious Chevi is deeply proud of her family's rich history, but she also feels she's paving her own path.

Chevi is a transgender woman who identifies as two spirit, which refers to people who have both a male spirit and a female spirit. Historically, in many Indigenous cultures, two-spirit people were looked upon with high regard and considered sacred. Chevi graduated in 2003 from Ponoka Composite High School and worked at various jobs in Ponoka. She then attended and graduated from the Hospitality, Tourism, and Management program at Red Deer College. Her talent for makeup artistry is a result of her attending and graduating from Marvel Hair College's Makeup Artistry program. Always wanting to learn more and to improve herself, Chevi also attended Maskwacis Culture College.

Like a caterpillar transitioning into a beautiful and strong butterfly, Chevi's metamorphosis happened when she was tragically assaulted in 2012. Though the experience shook her like nothing else, it didn't stop Chevi's transformation into a force to be reckoned with. Watch out world!

Chevi grew up in a very loving home with a supportive family and extended family as well as an accepting community. There's a stereotype that assumes that small towns are discriminatory against transgender people, but that's not necessarily true. Chevi felt supported and was hired by the Ponoka Chamber of Commerce businesses as an artist; her job was to decorate their windows for the local Ponoka Stampede. But when Chevi was attending the University of Alberta (for Native Studies and Economics), she was assaulted near campus.

"I always knew about discrimination," she says, "but it was always far. This was the first time it really entered my bubble, and it threw me off and shook me. I think that, at that time, I was in a vulnerable space. I had just gone through the breakup of a two-year relationship. Because of the breakup, I moved to the dorm from a condo in Leduc, Alberta. So I was in a vulnerable place when I was assaulted, and my boundaries were broken. When I was assaulted, I was just walking down the street, and my assailants started yelling at me. First they thought I was a girl. Then they stopped when they realized their mistake. They started swearing 'You're fucking gay!' and 'You're just a dude!' I waved at them, like, 'Thank you.' What was I supposed to do? There were all these people watching and wondering what was going on. Not only was it shocking, it was also humiliating. So that's where all my fear bottled up over time. I was humiliated in front of a lot of people and then assaulted. I think in that moment I thought of all the love and support I knew, and I knew the issue wasn't me—it wasn't my issue; it was theirs. It seems like so long ago.

"I kind of dealt with it quite a bit to get over it. I knew even back then that it wasn't my issue. It was more about their internalized homophobia. It was more about their ignorance. I was living a free and normal life. At the time, I was a makeup artist for Western Canada Fashion Week, and for Murel in West Edmonton

Mall. I also worked as a regional representative for L'Oreal, working for different departments, such as Hudson's Bay and Holt Renfrew. Within that makeup culture, it's totally normal to be self-expressive. I was doing my makeup, just doing my own thing. Went to get some groceries and was assaulted. It was close to the U of A (University of Alberta). I was leaving my dorm, walking down the street. Safeway is literally two blocks away from where I was living. I rented a house that was almost like a frat house, but it was just me living there. I went walking down the street and was literally assaulted. Really shocking. It threw me off, and I had to take some time off from school. I couldn't go to class. I started developing anxiety issues. Just stuff I was going through at the time; I didn't have names or labels for them. I just thought, 'Well, this isn't normal.' I thought, 'I can't go to class without panicking.' I became fearful, so I retreated back to Ponoka for a while and almost withdrew from school. I did end up withdrawing the following semester. That was a defining moment for me because I grew up with rose-coloured glasses. And the whole reason I went to the U of A in Native Studies, going through all these disciplines to find my passion, was so I could help First Nations.

"I think what shaped that worldview was growing up in Ponoka. In Maskwacis at the time there was a lot of oil money, so there was no social issues, no financial issues. When I looked at other First Nations groups, I was like, 'Why are they going through these issues? What's their problem?' So I thought that by going through Native Studies, I could help. I could help be a solution maker. I could find solutions, and I could do my part in helping and uplifting this community. That was my whole intention, and then I got assaulted. I became the person who needed help. I became the statistic. When I got assaulted, and all the news came in, all the influx came in, I realized that I was the 'Other.' I'm not part of the group; I'm considered the Other. That was a really defining moment, and it really shook my worldview because I grew up being so accepted. Then I started thinking, 'Am I really that different?' I'm native, LGBTQ, and I look different, so am I part of the underclass?

"It was the realization that this person assaulted me because there's this big group of people who actually think that's okay. It was really eye-opening. But it was also very uplifting because I spoke up. And from there I was able to speak up just because I thought 'This wasn't my fault.' A positive is the birth of the Hate to Hope campaign (which was founded by Chevi in 2012). It's finding my voice and speaking up, and realizing that I'm not alone. Not only is there a group of toxic people, there's also a lot of people going through similar issues who are voiceless. And then I realized that there are a lot of people going through trauma. It was a big learning lesson about rose-coloured glasses. Then Hate to Hope happened, and there's this story of me being different, and it's empowering because, wow, I'm not alone. There are a lot of people going through stuff. There are a lot of people who have been victimized, who have been silent. I thought this was a great opportunity. It seems to have hit a core with local society. It was also news in Canada, the U.S., Europe, and India. It seemed to resonate with a lot of people. I was like, 'Wow, there's been a whole lot of people who have been living in silence.' This was a defining moment that made me speak up even more.

"During that time, I was angry," Chevi continues. "When Hate to Hope was happening, it wasn't just about speaking up for silenced people. It was me saying, 'I'm angry! I'm really mad, and I've got to do something, this is not right!' At the moment I conceived Hate to Hope, it wasn't so much about helping anybody as it was about being really upset and knowing this wasn't right. I'm going to school, I'm living my life—this should not happen in the city. So I wanted to create safety-inclusive communities, and it kind of took on a life of its own. So, that's Hate to Hope in a nutshell. It's really big. It's all about safety-inclusive environments—that's what it morphed into. But, at the time, it was more about my own anger and letting everyone know that this is not okay."

I ask Chevi if friends and/or family made things better or worse for her in overcoming this tragedy. Chevi says they made it better and were an integral part of her support network. "I don't think I could have made it without them," she says. "Along with my supportive step-siblings, my mom was very supportive and very nurturing. I've always had friends who are very supportive. In school, I was almost bullied, but my friends stepped in. I've always built up solid groups of networks of friends. We trust each other, and we're going to support each other. It's unconditional love."

Does Chevi have a positive view of herself? Her confidence can be fluid, she says. Chevi grew up very confident in both her two-spirit gender and her ethnicity. But it's hard when society (magazines, social media, news, etc.) has so many labels for everyone, and sometimes it's hard to be comfortable with one's self. Sometimes it weighs on Chevi, but she works on being confident everyday. "I had a lot of self-doubt after the attack," she says. "I knew I was okay, but I also knew I changed a bit. I had to work on myself and my confidence in who I was. Just to reassure myself that I'm okay, because those people did rattle me to the core." It made Chevi doubt herself constantly as she asked herself if she really was so different as to deserve to be assaulted and humiliated. She knew she didn't deserve any of that, but her attackers obviously thought she did. So Chevi thought there must be some truth to it. But she couldn't reconcile these polar thoughts, leading her to more confusion and self-doubt.

As for now, "I'm very confident in who I am," Chevi says. "What I'm about. I know that everything I do is a lesson; everything I've gone through is a lesson. Sometimes it's a blessing in disguise. Sometimes I don't see it at the moment, but if I persevere through it, I actually get some really good life lessons from it."

When it comes to controlling her feelings and impulses, Chevi believes she has a good grip on them. "I would like to think so," she says. "But I think a lot of my creativity comes from those feelings and impulses, as a person. If I'm not (able to control her feelings), my impulses and instincts have led to good stuff before. In the past, if something instinctual happened, and I got emotional, I wrote things down or I would journal about it. Or I think of a different idea. But for my emotions, I think I've learned to manage them quite well. I have no choice." Though Chevi's impulses heightened after the attack, she feels being emotionally impulsive, if it's done properly and in a positive way, can produce some good things.

What about Chevi's problem solving and communication skills during difficult times? It depends on the situation, she says. If she understands the problem or situation, she has the confidence to try to solve it. This was evident when Chevi founded Hate to Hope to help other people. During difficult times, she feels the rawness and gravity of the situation. She knows she's going to have to make some tough choices and will have to be honest with herself. She can think things through internally, but sometimes she wants a different perspective, in which case she confides in friends and family. But she also understands that not all of her friends and family share the same life experiences as her and may have different worldviews and opinions. They haven't been in Chevi's shoes, so they can't fully understand what it feels like to be a double minority, to be victimized, or to speak up for others. So, if Chevi is going through a rough time, they may not fully understand and not have the answers she's looking for. Chevi also approaches friends to be part of a focus group so Chevi can ask them about their opinions and advice. She then looks at all the answers, rather like brainstorming, and can usually pick up a common theme in the responses.

I asked Chevi if she feels like she's in control of her life. "I feel like I'm in control," she says. "But when you look at the big picture, are any of us really in control? There are so many avenues of possibilities and careers. You can't really be in control of your life. You can't be like, 'Oh, I want to be a reality star!' or 'I wanna do this!' or 'I wanna be an artist!' You have to have the skills needed to do those things, so you have to look at your skill set; you have to look at what's available. Can you make money? Is it realistic? Are you contributing? So I think I'm in control of my responses to a certain point. But at a certain point, I still have to go to school. I still have to figure out what I want to do. I do think, though, that I'm in control of my choices for what's in front of me." In her bad moments, Chevi feels she's not in control, but she does try to control her outlook and her responses to the situation.

When encountering a bad situation, does Chevi feel like a victim? Or does she see the experience as a blessing in disguise? At the time of turmoil, Chevi says, it doesn't feel like the situation is a blessing in disguise, but she also feels she can learn from it. She sees it as a choice—she can either not learn from it and let it get under her skin and dictate her life, or she can use it as a lesson that will help her help others. Chevi gains confidence from getting through the negative experiences as well. And if she finds other people in the same situation, she can share her experiences to help them. She knows she needs to feel the pain and rawness of it to work through it and come out the other side. If she feels she can get through it unscathed, it's incredibly empowering for her. These are the kinds of rough experiences in life that you can't learn about in school.

What tools or coping mechanisms does Chevi use when going through rough times? When she was a child, she says, "My mother didn't understand because I was very different from others in the community we grew up in. I was always very artistic with a lot of self-expression. My mom didn't have the answers, so she gave me books. She gave me *Chicken Soup for the Teenage Soul*, all of them, the whole collection. In all of these books, she would highlight stuff for me to read as a teen. I have a library collection of all of them. In them she wrote little messages and highlighted things I didn't know the answer to. Things like, 'Why is this person making fun of me?' 'Why am I going through this?' All of those childhood issues, like trying to fit in. She would say, 'I don't know, but here's a book.' Reading those stories helped me understand myself because I was able to formulate my own responses. Instead of her telling me what to do and then me blaming her if it didn't work, I could actually get my own response from the books.

"I still read and develop my own answers," Chevi says. "So if I'm going through something tough, I read all these different self-help books and then come out with my own answers. So I basically read self-help books and quotes, do fine-art painting, and continue to be self-expressive. I just need a creative outlet; that's how I deal with stress." Chevi also likes to isolate herself at times and be alone to just reflect, which includes a lot of introspection. Chevi also finds that volunteering and helping others helps her. She feels better and less stressed when she's making a difference in someone else's life. Chevi does admit that she does sometimes cope in unhealthy ways, such as drinking too much. But she knows it's an unhealthy choice. "I learned through experience that when you have issues," she says, "it's the worst time to use alcohol."

How do Chevi's family and friends cope with stress? Her family copes by turning to their First Nations culture for connection. In the last five years, her mom, in particular, has turned to her culture as a source of connection to cope with stress. Her mom has always been a very spiritual person in her beliefs. Chevi's family also copes by helping others. During community events, her family does the volunteering for a potluck or a cultural activity. Conversely, they may also take time off during times of stress. Chevi's mom also turns to books or vacations.

And Chevi's friends? They're all very creative and support each other. They have a "focus group," where all the friends come together and listen to and support each other. It's a free and safe environment where everyone bounces ideas off each other and they are all honest with each other. Topics range from career choices, to love, to rainbow crosswalks. The feedback is real and not malicious. This kind of arrangement also exists within Chevi's family. They help each other brainstorm ideas if someone is struggling to find an answer. When Chevi gets the different responses or suggestions from family and friends about an issue, she thanks them and picks the one that's for her. They also help each other with creative projects to help alleviate heavy thoughts from their minds. For example, helping a friend campaign when running for Member of Parliament. Another example is their creative project that resulted in the first rainbow crosswalk on a First Nations reserve. It was all over the news. It was an important project for Chevi; she was feeling stressed at the time, but she also wanted to help out and give back to the community. She felt good about it because she was helping herself feel safe and helping the LGBTQ community in First Nations reservations as well. Equally important, Chevi let the community know that they have the support of someone just like them.

What does Chevi think about negative emotions as a sign of perseverance? "I see the value of this," she says. "I always say a painful situation makes or breaks people. It's a challenge you didn't want, but it's there, and it's painful. How you react to it is going to be a lesson, or it's going to test who you are. Some people, when pain comes in, will retreat and escape. They'll spend years turning to bad coping mechanisms, like drinking. They'll find different deflecting techniques to avoid that issue or that painful situation. Or they deflect it to something like Hate to Hope. When I think about the assault, I don't think of me; I think of Hate to Hope. Pain is growth. You need those struggles to really find out who you are and find your place in this world. You need the struggles to make you or break you, and not everybody can handle it. That's why people have addiction issues. They're not dealing with that pain."

Chevi doesn't believe there's such a thing as resilient people who aren't affected by stress. She believes there's a threshold, and that everybody's built differently. It depends on their upbringing and their experiences. Through experiences, some people build up a muscle of resilience over time. And some are brought to their knees by the weight of life's burdens. The resilient, however, know they've been in tough situations before, and they draw on their past struggles to make it through their present ones. As Chevi puts it: "I've been here before, and I can do it, and I can handle it. Maybe I can learn a new lesson. I don't want to be here, but I'm here, and I will be more resilient. I can be less emotional and less reactionary. In the last situation, I did this. But this time, I have more of a choice. I'm not going to detour and fall off."

Failure is an inevitable part of being human. In the face of failure, Chevi believes you need persistence, and you need to get back up: "You need perseverance because if you give up along the way, you're not going to learn the lesson. You're not going to learn about yourself. You're not going to learn introspection and you're going to run away. You're not going to see the best of who you can be. If you give up on the way, you give up when you're almost there.

The lesson may have gotten too tough for you, or your resilient muscle wasn't built up, but there's a danger you'll be stuck there forever. Some people get stuck there for life. I think if you push through and persevere, you get through the struggle. Then you'll look back and go, 'Wow, that was a good lesson.'

"But you have to fail sometimes. I think people who are resilient know what failure feels like. They know what success feels like, and they know what failure feels like. They know the struggle and all the hard work it takes to get to that point. That's what perseverance is—not giving up. Because if you give up, you'll never live to your fullest potential. You'll never really get to see what's out there. Me wanting to travel, for example. If I don't persevere and get to a point where I feel safe enough to travel, I'll never learn. I have to take myself to situations where I can learn. Just face it. Endure it. And say to yourself, 'These feelings are natural, and I validate them. These are my scary thoughts—are they real? Can I reframe this?' Even knowing that the fear is there, you keep on going anyway. You don't know all the answers, but you just know you don't want to be where you are, you don't want to feel how you feel, so you have to persevere."

Chevi feels we have a vision of our lives and what our lives should be. We have a lot of expectations from our parents, our employers, our peers, society, etc. And we put a lot of pressure on ourselves on top of that, which leads to frustration when things don't go our way. If you let that frustration imprison you, you limit yourself and your potential. We need to explore our potentials and self-development; if we succumb to life's adversities, we'll never see beyond the present moment and really know how full we can be. If we succumb, we're really limiting ourselves.

What other tools does Chevi use to help her get through difficult moments? Chevi relies on New Earth books to help her. She's spiritual, and believes in a higher being or higher power. Chevi keeps anything that resonates with her. This also applies to art books. If everything she's tried doesn't work, and Chevi finds herself really stuck in a rut, she will either bide her time and wait for a new opportunity to arise, go search for new opportunities, or just focus on present opportunities to live a fulfilling life. She knows she's not resistant all the time, but she also knows she'll need to be resilient, pick herself up, and move forward. She also does a self-inventory of how true to herself she is being by analyzing whatever decision she needs to make and following through with her decision. If she encounters a roadblock in her analysis, she looks at other options or opportunities that might provide the same results while still allowing her to be true to herself. "I reflect a lot," Chevi says. "I sit back and think about my life, and I interact with people. If I go beyond my values, I don't feel good. If I cross them, I don't feel good about myself. The choice I make has to align to my values; it has to align with who I am; it has to align with my beliefs."

Chevi shares some words of wisdom with others who are struggling: "It's going to be tough," she says. "Whatever is happening to you—whether it was unfair or unjust—you're going to be angry. But you're going to persevere and keep on moving because, at the end of the day, you're going to have to be happy with yourself, and you're going to have to move forward. Life is unfair. Life will get the best of you at times. But you're going to have to pick yourself up no matter what. Because no one else is going to do it for you. You can have the biggest support network in the world, but you have to make that effort. Be honest with yourself, and don't sugar coat the mistakes, the tribulations, the letdowns; be honest with yourself. Seek out help, talk to people you trust. Build up those support networks. Talk to your friends and family. Read books. Do art. Do stuff that makes you happy. You have to do the work. You have to educate yourself. Human connection is at the core of everything. Don't completely isolate yourself, because that's the worst thing you can do. Through all of my difficult situations, I've kept talking to my friends and family. Or maybe do some volunteer work. Just go out there, and don't give up on yourself—know that it will get better; everything is temporary."

Dancing Queen

Bailey Dunbar was born in St. John, New Brunswick, lived in Fort McMurray, Alberta for about two years, and has now been living in Fort Saskatchewan, Alberta for three years. The 17 year old has had quite a physical journey for someone of such a young age. It has also been a continuous personal journey of losing and finding herself over and over again. Bailey's courage to stand up time and time again after being knocked down countless times is a true testament of human resiliency in the dance of life. Sometimes she follows, but most of the time she tries to lead, step-by-step.

On June 27, 2014, Bailey's world turned upside down in a way most of us can't even imagine. Bailey lost her identical twin sister, Morgan, to suicide. Bailey and her parents came home after spending a day out and found Morgan in the bedroom that Bailey and Morgan shared. "After Morgan had passed away," Bailey says, "that's when the depression set in for me. I hadn't really been eating for a couple of months, and then I started falling for really bad habits like drugs, drinking, and smoking. That carried on for some time. It was the first day of the summer after we were in Grade 6 that she passed away.

"Up until Grade 8, I had a really bad drug habit with drinking and smoking. Grade 8 is when my parents found out about it. That's when they decided to take it on, to help me. During the beginning of the Grade 8 year, I ended up trying to get off of my medication, which I'm still on now. I ended up having a mental break where I tried to kill myself at school. The vice principal had to drive me to the hospital. I don't remember anything from that day. But apparently the doctors said that my vital signs were very fatal, and I should have died. But they still treated me.

"So that was my break—and the point at which I realized that I was actually hurting. It was probably depression, PTSD, and anxiety that contributed to my suicide attempt. I was still in my drug phase, but not as bad, coming into Grade 9. I quit fully after I left Grade 9. In December 2016, I ended up having another mental breakdown and tried to kill myself again, but I was at home this time. A policeman ended up showing up at the door, because I had told my boyfriend at the time that I was going to kill myself. He called the police to come and check on me. And that's when I left school and began home schooling. I finished the rest of Grade 9 at home with my mom. That's when I realized that school was the main issue contributing to the drug habit and all the stress on my shoulders. Then I realized that I needed to focus more on dance."

When Bailey lived in Fort McMurray for two years, she found her hidden talent and her love for hip-hop dancing. So she joined a hip-hop group in Fort McMurray and another one in Fort Saskatchewan. She did hip-hop for two years, and recently began exploring intensive dance, which includes a variety of dances, such as ballet, musical theatre, hip-hop, lyrical, jazz, and tap.

After Grade 9 ended, Bailey focused more on dance and schooling (still from home). When it was time to go to high school, she didn't want to go to the local high school because of people she had issues with. Bailey and her mom found the perfect solution in Next Step High School in Fort Saskatchewan, and Bailey also got involved with the dance community again and danced four days a week.

"But as soon as I got into high school," Bailey says, "I realized high school is a lot of work and stress. Besides that, I would go to the dance studio, and I soon realized that a lot of people there didn't like me because I came from a performance hip-hop group and then joined all these different types of styles and I caught on pretty quickly. My flexibility was natural. So a lot of people weren't... I don't know how to word it. They weren't happy that I was able to do that. When I entered my second year of intensive high school, a lot of people kept putting more stress on me by starting rumors about me at the dance studio. It put so much stress on me that it was getting to the point that I was so stressed out about school and dance that I was feeling suicidal again. So, I had to make a choice to quit the one thing I loved most to focus on myself. It broke my heart; it really did. But I had to do it because I had to look after myself—if I had continued going, I would have ended up in the hospital again. And I didn't want to put my parents through that, or my boyfriend at the time, because he knew everything about me. We started dating in November after meeting in September at Next Step. I had already had one setback where I cut myself a few times at school. He was the one to bring me outside and calm me down. He broke down and cried, and that broke my heart. And I realized that people love me. I can't leave them, so here I am."

I asked Bailey if friends and family helped or made things worse after Morgan's death. "Honestly," she says, "I lost a lot of friends. And then I gained new friends. My original friends—the ones I've known since Grade 1 in New Brunswick—have helped me a lot since Morgan died. Once Morgan died, they realized that we were all growing up.

"A lot of my original friends back home—ones I still keep in contact with—helped me through it. But the toxic friends I had up in Fort McMurray and in Fort Saskatchewan made it harder for me. Instead of trying to be there for me and support me through what I was going through, they ended up manipulating me into doing other things rather than trying to be a better person. Like doing drugs; instead of telling me that that was not what I needed, they would tell me it was my medication.

"My family went through hell and back," Bailey continues. "I do have other siblings. I have two older sisters in New Brunswick. My oldest sister has two children, and my second oldest sister has one. My brother is currently in Fort McMurray but, unfortunately, he's a drug addict. So I don't get to see him much. He's only 20 or 21 years old, and he's been a drug addict since he was 12 years old. That's hard on me too. But Morgan's death was hard on him as well. He came to the hospital, and he broke down crying. It broke my heart to see my brother cry. But I can't really help him if he can't help himself."

Self-confidence can be hit and miss for Bailey: "I can be confident sometimes, like right now I'm confident. But at the same time, I'm nervous and scared, like I'm going to say the wrong thing. And with public speaking, I'm confident before I start speaking, but as soon as I start to speak, I stutter and get worried, and that's when my anxiety takes over. But I've definitely gained a lot more confident throughout the years; I know that. My mom has helped me a lot with that. Same with school—as much as I don't want to admit it, school has helped me with public speaking because of the projects. But yeah, I'm kind of like 50-50. It depends. I'm confident, but at the same time I'm nervous."

Does Bailey have control over her feelings and impulses? "No, not always," she admits. "Actually, toward the end of Grade 8, in April, when I still had my drug habit, I ended up going out with the wrong guy. I ended up being raped. I didn't tell my parents at first, not until the beginning of Grade 9, when he eventually said something wrong to me, and I actually let my emotions take over; I threatened him and told him that if he ever came near me again, I would hurt him. And that was another reason I had to leave Grade 9. As soon as I got into Next Step in Grade 10, I was doing fine, until one day he decided to come to the school because he was going to go there for high school. Instead of being a mature person and kind of ignoring it, I ended up waiting until his mom went into an office to talk to the vice principal, and I punched him. So, yes, I let my emotions control me sometimes."

When it comes to using or not using problem solving and communication skills, Bailey says, "I'm kind of both. It's got to the point where if I'm going to have a mental break, and I know I'm going to either hurt myself or others, I know to tell someone about it or call someone I trust to help me. But there are still times when I don't know when to seek help. I'm older now, and I do know my triggers, and I do know when my anxiety attacks are going to happen, or when I'm going to have flash backs about Morgan's death because of my PTSD, or when I'm really depressed, and I don't want to do anything but stay in bed all day. I still force myself to get up and do things, and I try to push the negatives out of the way, but there are still days when I just don't want to do anything, and I don't want anyone to help me; I just want to do nothing."

Bailey feels she has control of her life only sometimes—sometimes she does, and sometimes she doesn't, she says. She's young and still has to listen to her parents, so they have some control over her life. But there are some days where she feels she could take on the adult life. It really depends on the day.

During difficult moments, does her experience make Bailey feel like a victim, or does she see the moment as an opportunity to grow and become a stronger person? "It depends on the situation," Bailey says. "With Morgan's death, I saw my family and I as victims of her dying because she passed on her pain to us. But, at the same time, it did make me into a stronger person—it shaped me into who I am, and that's especially true for my family as well. But honestly, it really depends on the situation I'm in. When Morgan died, I realized a lot of people suffer from depression and mental health issues. And someone affected should be able to speak out about what they went through and what they're going through at the moment and just share their voice. I honestly see that as an opportunity as well."

To cope with stress during tough times, Bailey listens to music or dances through it. Or she'll try to focus on memorizing lyrics to a song. But she mostly turns to dance to get through rough times because dance was a major part of her life for four years. As for how Bailey's friends and family cope with stress, Bailey says, "My parents cope with stress by working out. I usually tend to dance, listen to music, or read. I don't read as much anymore. I usually stress eat too, which is really bad. But I tend to dance a lot to cope. As for my friends back home, it's hard to say. I know my best friend uses his favorite sport, badminton, to cope with stress. My other friend hangs out with a group of other friends where everyone has known everyone else since Grade 1. These friends all hang out with each other to calm each other down. My boyfriend plays video games to cope with stress better. He'll also talk to me right away. As soon as he's upset or stressed, he'll call me."

Negative emotions can lead to spiritual growth and provide a learning experience. As Bailey says, "If you have negative feelings, use them. Use them to make yourself grow stronger. Use them to define yourself. My PTSD and depression define me in that I'll see something that triggers me, and people will think it's funny. I just tell them I can't help it. It's me. That's how it is, and I can't help it, and I'm not going to change it. I'm not ashamed of it. I just accept it as fact."

I asked what Bailey's thoughts are on resilient people being immune to stress. "Deep inside, everyone is the same," she says. "Inside or outside, disability or not. I find everyone is the same inside. We all have labels now. It's 2018—we all have different types of labels and different ways we see each other and different names we call each other. But really, on the inside, we're human. All is equal."

Perseverance is an important concept to mental health. It provides motivation during our darkest times. "Keep going," Bailey says on this subject. "No matter how many times you fail. Nobody is going to get it perfect on the first try. If you really want to succeed, you have to take all the chances you can take. Look at pro hockey stars or basketball players; look at how many times it took them to get really good at making good shots or doing certain tricks. They definitely didn't get it right on their first try. Same with gymnasts or dancers. Say if you're a dancer and you can't do four pirouettes in a row, you can only do two. You're not going to give up right then, right? If you're going to do four, you're not going to do it right away; you've got to work for it. But you've got to be easy and kind to yourself too."

Bailey looks into the future and wonders what it's going to be like being a crane operator (a dream of Bailey's), or what it'll be like once she gets married and has a house. She has a number of goals to look forward to. Instead of having a big lofty plan, she has little plans or little snippets of those plans or goals to work toward. She has a job now, and she plans to save up for more tattoos. She looks forward to it. Bailey has come a long way and continues to look forward in finding herself over and over again by setting up little goals and going from there. Because that's all you can do, sometimes.

It wasn't hard to come up with the title for Bailey's chapter. As soon as I heard her story, I saw Bailey as the Dancing Queen in ABBA's hit song. I can see Bailey dancing towards her future. It may not be easy, but as ABBA put it,

> *You are the Dancing Queen*
> *Young and sweet, only seventeen*
> *Dancing Queen*
> *Feel the beat from the tambourine*
> *Oh yeah*
> *You can dance, you can jive*
> *Having the time of your life, oh*
> *See that girl, watch that scene*
> *Digging the Dancing Queen.*

"It gets better," Bailey says. "It really does. I'm in a really good place compared to four years ago when Morgan died. At the same time, I'm still in a rough place. There will still be urges to smoke, but I know I can't do it. I still get urges to want to kill myself, but I can't do it because I've got goals that I've set and want to achieve. I want to reward myself with that. I want to see new stuff in the world, like new music to discover or new dances to discover, new items, everything. I'm just very much that type who wants to discover a lot of things. But to the people who are going through a rough time right now and want to kill themselves and just end it all … it gets better, really. If you try to kill yourself, it's only going to make it worse. Trust me, I know. It's okay to let people know how you're feeling. It's definitely okay to try to talk to someone about it. And honestly, getting help is one of the best solutions."

The Unstoppable Dan Johnstone

A Canadian philanthropist, activist, community organizer, and humanitarian, it's only appropriate that Dan was bestowed with the nickname "Can Man Dan." Since 2011, Dan has travelled around Alberta helping the province's most vulnerable by raising millions for different endeavours and charities, such as food banks, the homeless community, and women's shelters. He also works to provide school supplies for low-income families and toys for children. Anywhere a need exists, Dan is there. He has never made money from any of these endeavours. "I believe it's more important to help people and do it from the goodness of your heart," he says.

To understand how Dan became this superhero (because not all superheroes wear capes) for Alberta's most vulnerable, we need to understand his childhood.

I first read about Dan a few years ago in our local newspaper. Such a young man doing such good deeds for so many in Alberta. What?! Why? Who does this?! My first impression was that he must have had quite an incredible experience when he was young that shaped him into someone so amazing. Nobody just wakes up one morning and decides to make the world a better place without some motivation behind it. I don't hear or see anybody else doing what Dan is doing at that level. If I read about someone doing something similar, it's usually someone who's retired and has a lot of time (and money) on their hands and decides they want to make the world a better place. Or it's someone who has started a non-profit, but the non-profit is affiliated with their start-up. You get the picture. The only other young activists comparable to Dan are Canadian brothers and children's rights advocates Marc and Craig Kielburger, who founded the We Charity (a children's charity founded in 1995). You may be familiar with one of their amazing initiatives called "We Day," which was created to empower, educate, and inspire. I read about what inspired the Kielburger brothers to do such good deeds for society, and part of it was that their mother took them to feed the homeless and introduced the boys to that world when they were very young. Obviously, they never forgot about it.

But what inspired our superhero Dan?

Dan's childhood wasn't a typical one. For most of his childhood, he lived in a single-parent household. His father left the family when Dan was very young. His mom, Pamela Johnstone, was left to take care of the family. She worked hard and always held two to three jobs, all at minimum wage, as she tried to keep things together. Before Dan's brother Michael was born, his mom was involved in a series of unhealthy relationships.

"They were tough years," Dan says. "There was a lot of domestic abuse, drug use, and alcohol use. And poverty. It was very systemic. It was like something you would see on television. You watch these poor families growing up—that was my reality. My mom always said that I grew up quicker than most kids. It's because I really had to take the role of … well, not quite raising myself, because my mom, regardless of her issues, was still a great mother. But it was tough because I would see my mom high or drunk or being abused. It was stuff like that. And then, of course, affording food was always an issue when paying the bills. And eating sometimes meant no electricity and stuff. So I grew up and went to elementary school, and I literally started working when I was 11 or 12 years old. I was delivering flyers just to make ends meet."

Looking back, Dan wishes he had had more time for school. But survival was a priority, and desperate times called for desperate measures. There was no choice: "Marks are very important," Dan says. "But I couldn't do it. I would go to school when I could, but sometimes I couldn't go to school because there was no food in the house for weeks, so I would miss school for weeks on end. I also had to go to work both before school and after school."

It didn't make it easier when Michael's father became abusive toward their mother. That experience has turned Dan into an activist against domestic violence, and he has supported many women's shelters through his philanthropic initiatives throughout the years.

"I lived with him," Dan says, referring to Michael's father. "I saw my mom get beat up and locked in the closet and locked away while hurt. I'll never forget those memories, and that's why I help women and children who are in the same position." Dan's childhood wasn't conventional to say the least, but it has made Dan the person he is today. He transfers all that has happened and all the energy associated with it into his current initiatives. Because of his upbringing, he's raised millions of dollars through his initiatives to help Alberta's most vulnerable community.

I think we can all agree that, during adolescence, the endless angst, anxiety, and self-doubt associated to that phase of our lives is a trying time. But for Dan, it was even harder because of his experiences at home: "There was a point for awhile where I saw my friends with their normal families. I was so envious of what they had, and I wished I had that. Looking back now, though, I'm okay with everything. Everything turned out. It's just the randomness of life. It is what it is, and you just have to accept it."

Dan and his mom have a great relationship. She helps Dan with his initiatives in the community. Considering there are so many broken families with fractured relationships, Dan has a pretty wonderful family that is supportive of him. And that's what family is, however we define *normal*.

I asked Dan if his family and/or friends make it easier or harder for him in overcoming his childhood experiences: "I've never been one to confide in anybody," Dan says. "I think it's just more or less me accepting what happened and moving on with my life. I didn't go to therapy and I didn't talk to friends about it. Not even my family. Everyone tried talking to me about it, because it was obviously a traumatic upbringing, but I've accepted it. Honestly, to this day, it doesn't ... well, I've come to terms with it. It was part of my life. It was my past, and now is the future."

Thanks to his mom, Dan sees himself as a pretty confident person. She taught Dan to straighten up, stand tall, and hold his head high. "Being the poor kid in school, and wearing not last season's clothes, but clothes from, like, five seasons ago, I was bullied. And, of course, being a minority, I was bullied. But my mom taught me to rock it. To just have that confidence.

"I've always sort of, you know, put myself on a different level than other people. But not because I'm an egomaniac. My confidence is there, but I don't lower myself to the petty name-calling. This is true even to this day, because a lot of people are still super petty. If you don't like me, that's fine. You don't have to like me. I'll just move on. Life's too short to stick around and argue with people and try to prove yourself to people. Maybe because I'm a public figure, I have my haters. I go into interviews and people disagree with me completely. And I'm okay with that. I'm not here on this planet to try to change their opinions. If my actions and my words don't speak loud enough, I'm not going to sit there and try to change their minds about me. I'm always on my own little plane, and I just move forward."

Does Dan feel he has control over his feelings and impulses? Most of his friends, supporters, and even the naysayers, say he's an emotional person. He always wants to help those in distress, perhaps because he can relate. He is who he is, and isn't trying to be anybody else anytime soon. If Dan sees something he doesn't agree with, he doesn't clam up and hope it goes away or gets better on its own. He tries to do something about it. He knows he's an emotional person, and he's proud of it.

When Dan faces an uphill battle of any sort, he says, "I'm someone who harbours it for as long as I can. I don't want anyone to be concerned about me, and I don't want people to go out of their way to help me. I just … I'm a very personal person. There are three people in my life I tell my issues to. And, unless they're in that small group, no one will have any idea that I'm going through things. I've always been a very, very private person. This may be a downfall one day, but I rarely confide in anyone who's not my friend. Sometimes it hurts me, but I'm not a big believer in complaining. Maybe it's the way I've been raised. You can complain all you want, but we're still going to be poor. You go out there and make a difference. That's the mentality I have. You work with what you've got, and you do your best with it."

Dan doesn't feel he has control of his life, but that's not as bad as it sounds. He feels life is random and mysterious, and he believes it's not up to him how his life will turn out, no matter how good of a person he tries to be. That may come across as religious, but Dan says he has become more spiritual than religious. If you've ever heard the expression, "If you want to make God laugh, tell him about your plans," this applies to how Dan sees life. But that's not going to stop him from living, having fun, and dodging life's curve balls. Buckle up and enjoy the ride (yes, even when it gets bumpy!).

"I never feel like a victim," Dan says. "As we've discussed, life is just—it is what it is—a big ball of randomness. I never look for an opportunity for a lesson to be taught to me, or seek out something I can gain from. Lessons are learned throughout life, but I don't go into a serious or negative situation and think, 'Okay, what can I learn from this?' It might come to me a year later or 10 years later. I just take the punches as they come. I counter where I can, and if I see someone else taking the punches, I lend a hand. I don't really go into 'learning things' because it's constantly changing. Eight billion people—something is bound to affect you. It is what it is. I wake up every morning, and I live that day, and I go to bed again, and I wake up again, and I live *that* day."

Dan feels the experiences he had during his childhood were a blessing in disguise. It made him into the man he is today. He's out there doing great things, such as travelling the province helping thousands of people in crisis.

When it comes to getting through tough times, Dan says, "It all depends on what stage I'm at in my life. There was a time I turned to prayer. That helped me greatly. Talking to God." I asked him if he still prays. "No, no," he says. "It's funny; I still take my mom to church because she's very religious. And religion is a whole different conversation because it's so big. I'm not as religious as I should be. You know, one day I'll come to regret that when I'm at the pearly gates.

"But when I'm really worked up and I'm upset, maybe I'll work out, maybe I'll post on social media. But even that is very rare. I really just like to be alone. I turn on some classical music, and I literally just go away for a bit. One of my biggest stress relievers in life is to go to a theatre by myself and get all this junk food and just eat it. I watch the movie for two or three hours, and I come out de-stressed. Then I put on some classical music, and I'm on my way. I kind of disappear for a while from, like, anybody. I don't read inspirational stuff, I don't pray anymore, and I don't talk to anybody. It's just that I need to come to terms with what's in front of me on my own, and once that happens, I'm back to normal."

I asked Dan how his friends and family cope with stress. Dan says that his mom and brother still haven't made peace with the past. His mom still has nightmares about what happened to her and her family. She can advise Dan that he can't change the past and should move on, but she struggles to believe it herself. Dan's brother Michael is the same. His mom and Michael are very similar in this regard. His mom and Michael do talk to each other a lot about what happened, and they talk to Dan about it as well. Dan's mom and Michael go to group therapy, but Dan doesn't like that environment. Some people find talking to someone very therapeutic. For Dan, it's the total opposite. He just wants to be alone.

Before I could even finish asking Dan if negative emotions can be beneficial to one's personal or spiritual growth, he agreed. "I remember my past and I embrace it," he says. "I know there's a lot of negative memories and negativity, but I still use that to build my character today. I don't forget, and I don't let a lot of things go, but I do forgive. Still, I always carry these memories and baggage with me because it helps shape me as a person. Also, I think my experiences can help someone else. I never ever want to forget where I came from because it seems very counterproductive. This is your journey, this is your story, and you should always remember it. And work on not repeating it. So I never forget, but I do forgive."

When it comes to his thoughts about resilient people never having to deal with stress, Dan says that many of his friends and family actually think Dan himself is one of those people. Sometimes he gets worked up or emotional about things, but he never gets to the breaking point. He doesn't get rattled or fazed easily. Life has thrown Dan a lot of curve balls since he was a kid, but guess what? He's still standing, he's still here, and he's unstoppable!

Dan shares how his mom used to be the strongest person he knew, despite her troubled and challenging childhood. But it seems to have caught up to her, and she struggles with the memories of it. "I don't think anybody is immune to stress," Dan says. "I think it will always be there, but it's about how you handle it and, eventually, what you do with it. There will come a time where you become tired of handling it. Life is really not fair for some people, and maybe you get so tired of dealing with it. And maybe you see so many emotional breakdowns, mental breakdowns, or health deterioration. Sometimes life weighs on you, and you crumble. I don't think anybody is immune to it. I think it just affects people differently. I think the really lucky people get to avoid the stress ball for the most part. But I think it will affect everybody at some point eventually."

Dan feels strongly that the whole mental health industry is under-researched and under-developed. With respect to the many people in his life and from the general population who are experiencing mental illness, he feels it's become an epidemic. And it's not a recent phenomenon that has just creeped it's head out of the woodwork like the long-lost relatives of lottery winners. It's always been there, but nobody wanted to talk about it, and there was less social and medical awareness about it. With the help of social media, mental health and mental illness is finally getting the attention it deserves.

"You can't persevere through your mental health issues; you just can't," Dan says. "That's just the stupidest mentality, and I'm sorry if you believe that. I went to church to pray it away. But no, you can't pray it away or persevere through it. You need help! Whether it's someone to talk to or medication, you need some sort of support. Nobody has really taken it seriously until the last two or three years. I'm excited about the research that'll be done in the next decades because I think we'll find a lot of brain patterns and wavelengths. I look forward to the future because, right now, it's just a blip on the radar. We see it, but let's get closer to it and actually study it. But yeah, there's no persevering, and there's no praying it away. If you need the support, get the support. I don't care if you call one of those 1-800 numbers at 2 a.m., book a doctor's appointment, or just go get *some* sort of support."

Inspirational quotes work fine for a day or as the mantra for one's life, Dan says, but he himself doesn't find any use for them. He does feel, however, that if they do help someone, that's great. Quotes are fun, he says, but they're a short-term solution, not something you can base how you live your life on.

Another tool Dan uses to feel better when going through a difficult time is helping others. Some of you may not know it, but Dan was voted "Best Activist" in *Vue Weekly's* "Best of Edmonton 2017," and "Edmonton's Favourite Philanthropist" for 2018. He was also recently a recipient of *Avenue Magazine's* 2018 "Top 40 Under 40" award. Wowsa!

His passion and initiatives, through Can Man Dan, all center on helping the less fortunate and some of the most vulnerable populations in our province.

And he's been doing this since 2011. "It's very therapeutic," he says. "You go out and you buy these things, whether it's backpacks or school supplies or meals for people, or whatever. You see people with real issues and real problems and it makes your problems seem that much smaller. You realize how tiny your problems are.

"I mean, some of these people have no homes, or they're going to lose their house, or they can't afford food that night, and the kids are running around with no school supplies or Christmas gifts. You feel bad, and you say, 'I'm having a bad day, but it's not as bad as what's happening over there.'"

I recently witnessed first-hand Dan doing this when he was going through some rough times. Where most people would succumb to or be brought to their knees by the pressures or darkness of life, Dan distributed food hampers to families who needed it, spoke to kids in schools about homelessness, and supported local businesses. Dan looked life in the eyes and said, "Sorry life! Can't stop me that easily!" Spoken like a true, and unstoppable, warrior.

Dan offers these words of wisdom for people going through difficult times: "I'm not a doctor or a therapist. Nobody knows you better than you. If you need help, ask somebody for it. Even though I can live with my issues, and I can make them disappear after a few hours, a lot of people can't do that. It's important for you to have an outlet—somewhere where you can let that stress out—because if you carry it for too long, it's going to break you down.

"I think it's important that everyone have that person, that place, or that area they can go to, whether it's God, meditation, friends or family, or a movie theatre. Make sure you're always taking time to decompress; life will honestly wear on you after a long time because we're moving so quickly. A lot of people are forgetting to take that time and de-stress. It's very vital and important. I don't give advice because I'm not really authorized to, but make sure you take time for yourself, realize what you're capable of and who you are, and make sure you have an outlet for that negativity."

Attitude of Gratitude

Brittney Neunzig was born and raised in Grimshaw, Alberta, Canada. She has been married to her husband, Joe, for seven years. They have two children (their nine-year-old son Jacob is in Grade 4, and their five-year-old daughter Jamie is in Kindergarten). Along with her busy family life, Brittney runs a non-profit from home and is also a substitute teacher. Pretty ordinary lady, you may think. Make that a pretty extraordinary lady.

When Brittney was almost 14 years old, she was in a snowmobile accident: "(It) left me paralyzed from the chest down. The accident happened on December 2nd. I was invited to go snowmobiling. I had just moved. Actually, I had moved away from Grimshaw for a few years, and had just moved back. I had just started school and made some friends and got invited to go snowmobiling. It was sort of the thing for the young boys to do. We usually went snowmobiling in town, which sounds really weird, but there's an area called the 'drainage ditch.' It's behind some houses, and there's an open field there. We usually went there. So I asked my mom if I could go. She didn't really want me to, but she finally said okay after I sort of worn her down a little bit.

"So I went snowmobiling with my friends, and when I got to where we were to meet, the boys decided they wanted to go out to one of their acreages, which was like 30 kilometers out of town. I can't remember if they wanted to show me something or go get somebody, or what it was that made them want to go out that far. I was kind of like, 'Um, I don't know if my mom would want me to snowmobile that far.' There was no adult supervision or anything, but I didn't want to say no because I had just moved there. Also, there was a boy I liked there, so I really wanted to go. So I said 'Yeah, sure.' I didn't phone my mom because she would have told me to just come home and wouldn't have let me go. So I didn't call my mom, and I decided to go."

What happened next changed Brittney's life forever.

There were four boys, all 14 years old and two girls, both 13 years old. They all snowmobiled to the farm in question. They all got to the farm and talked for a bit. Brittney then switched snowmobiles with one of the boys, Blake Maddon, who was driving. She had been riding with another boy named Corey. Brittney got on Blake's snowmobile and gave her helmet to the other girl who was there because there weren't enough helmets for everyone. Off they went, and that was the last thing Brittney remembers.

"What I've been told from the friends who were there," Brittney explains, "is that the group lost track of us somewhere, and they were wondering where we were. They started looking for us, and we were sort of in the area where I grew up. If you go a bit further than Grimshaw, there's a town called Peace River, which the Peace River runs through. It's a large valley, and we were snowmobiling in those valley hills." Brittney's friends found her and Blake at the bottom of one of those valley hills. Luckily, Brittney was conscious and awake, but she wasn't coherent and doesn't remember much. Blake was conscious too. "They found us flipped upside down with the snowmobile on top of Blake and I," Brittney says. "So they lifted the snowmobile off of us. My face was really bloody because I wasn't wearing a helmet. And when we landed, Blake's helmet must have hit my nose. My nose was bleeding, and I was really scratched up. So I looked like I was really hurt. I kept saying, 'I can't feel my legs.' But Blake didn't look hurt at all, even though he was very hurt. He had a lot of internal injuries, and they didn't actually realize that."

Brittney's friends tried their best to get her up the hill, even though she had a spinal cord injury. One of the boys snowmobiled to a house to call an ambulance. The kids were in such a remote area that they had trouble guiding the ambulance in. But the adrenaline kicked in, and the boys did an amazing job of guiding the first responders to Brittney and Blake as soon as possible.

Tragically, Blake passed away while help was on the way. He had too much internal bleeding, but nobody knew that. "It was a really devastating accident for our town because it was a really small town of about 2600 people and just one high school," Brittney says. "I ended up being paralyzed from the chest down. I broke what they refer to as your T8 vertebrae. The top is cervical, and there are seven cervical vertebrae. The middle is the T—the 'Thoracic'—and the bottom is L—the 'Lumbar'—and then there's your tailbone. I broke T6. There are 12 Thoracic vertebrae, and I broke T6. So right in the middle, mid-chest level and a little farther down. There was also swelling and stuff. My function level is T6. I broke T8, but my function level moved up a little bit because of the swelling."

When the tear in Brittney's aorta was healed, and her brain swelling went down, she was transported to the University of Alberta (U of A) Hospital to have her spine operated on. "That's where I remember waking up—at the U of A," Brittney says. "I don't really remember much there other than a couple of people from my school bringing me teddy bears and a bunch of stuff and sitting with me. One of my clearest memories I have from there was when they kept telling me I was paralyzed. I was like 'What?' Because some people who become paralyzed get 'Phantom Sensation,' and I have that. So it always feels to me like my legs are bent and tingling; that, my doctor explained to me, is just basically the last thing your brain remembers feeling. It just sort of plays in a loop, over and over and over again. It always feels like that." Brittney didn't know she couldn't feel her legs anymore. Perhaps her brain couldn't register the trauma that had occurred. What shocked Brittney was when a physiotherapist came to see her: "She lifted up my leg to exercise it, and that was the first time I realized that the leg she was lifting was mine, and I couldn't feel it."

When asked how her friends and family helped her with her healing journey, Brittney says she was fortunate that she had good support throughout all the important transitions in her life after the accident. This helped with her self-esteem and helped her manage her emotions as well.

"I think relationships were huge for me," Brittney says. "When I was paralyzed, I remember having these thoughts, like, not that I was terrible, but simple thoughts, like, 'no boy will want to marry me,' or that kind of stuff. But, as it happened, the boy that I actually went snowmobiling for and I started dating right after I was paralyzed. He basically called me every day in the hospital, and he came to visit me. He was sort of my lifeline. I was really close with my sister—and this is sort of like the sad part of my story—but when I got paralyzed, for some reason, our relationship got really bad. I think it was because I clung to my boyfriend, Thomas, at the time as my lifeline. I was scared my friends would think I wasn't good enough anymore. It was sort of like I was at that age where friends mattered more than anything, and I was sort of mad at her (my sister) because she got to do all the teenage things I wanted to do. I don't remember internalizing that, but now as an adult, I think that might be what happened. So yes, relationships were key. I don't think I would have been as confident if I hadn't had that relationship with my boyfriend. He was with me all the time. We actually dated for seven years, until I moved out of the house and went to university."

Brittney's mom, Teresa Dodds, also played a huge support role for Brittney and reminded Brittney to always be grateful for what she had. Her mom was also an incredible support for Brittney in helping her manage the daily logistics of personal care for a paraplegic. "At the time," Brittney says, "I felt it was super helpful. In hindsight, though, I wish she had been a little harder on me, because it took me awhile to become independent."

In any event, Brittney's mom has always been Brittney's rock during the toughest of times. She was with Brittney at the hospital for the entire time (two weeks at the U of A and three months at the Glenrose Rehabilitation Hospital). "She always made me think about Blake, and how I still had a life to live. So, don't take it for granted. She used to say, 'Get up and do your physio,' and all that kind of stuff. She's also funny. We used to laugh a lot, and she made me keep things in perspective."

Brittney's cousin Melissa was also an integral part of Brittney's life after the accident. Melissa made sure Brittney got home safe and emotionally lifted Brittney up if she needed it. After the accident, the two became so much closer. Brittney had her boyfriend and her cousin/best friend with her most of the time, so it was a very strong support system.

When she was around other people, Brittney's confidence level was never much of an issue for her, but it was still difficult at times. It's always a required effort on her part, and isn't as easy as it sounds. "It's something I still struggle with all the time," Brittney says. "I don't know if it will ever go away. I imagine what I would do in the same situation if I weren't paralyzed. If I'm in a social situation or in a work situation, or whatever it is, I imagine myself in that same situation, but not paralyzed. And I imagine myself being more confident, or imagine the situation being easier. I struggle with that a lot. That being said, I don't let those struggles get in the way of things I want to do. So, even if I struggle with that, I know that's something I have to keep quiet all the time. I don't know if it will ever go away. I think I'm pretty confident, but I have to work at it."

Is Brittney someone who has a good handle on her feelings and impulses? To a certain extent, Brittney says: "It definitely depends on who I'm with. I have certain people who are always a soft place to fall. (My husband would be, like, 'I'm that guy!') So if I'm ever frustrated, or if I ever have a bad day, or I think 'Oh, this is so annoying!' he's the person I turn to first. For example, there are occasions where I go to my kids' school, and it's not wheelchair accessible, or I'll be wheeling around in the winter and someone hasn't shovelled properly, things like that. Certain things will get to me, and he's the one I will come home to and be like, 'Arg! I can't stand this!' But, to the rest of the world, I try to express an attitude of gratitude all the time. But that's definitely not 100% of the time."

When Brittney goes through rough times in her life, she tries to reach out for help. She does get overwhelmed and stressed quite easily, but she doesn't let the situation break her. "I'm not too proud to ask somebody who has also been there for help," she says. "I have friends or other people I know who are going through the same thing—I have other friends who are in wheelchairs. I'm definitely not too proud to express something that's frustrating me, to see if they've encountered the same situation and what they've done about it.

"That's part of the reason I want to start a blog; I believe that's how people gain the skills they gain—from seeing other people do things. And if they don't have an example, it's just a little more difficult." When Brittney was younger, she didn't have any role models and didn't know anyone else who was in a wheelchair and was successful—someone she could look up to. She didn't have anybody to confide in as she learned to handle certain situations.

But when she moved to the city, everything changed for Brittney: "I saw people who were living successful, happy, great lives. I've sort of been able to take their message of, 'You don't have to do it my way, but you will find a way,' and I ran with it. I've been able to sort of do that ever since. I feel like I'm good at problem solving. I've had two kids, which was pretty scary, but I've been able to do a lot of things in the parenting realm and sort of share my message with other people."

Brittney feels she has a good sense of control over her life. She strongly believes in energy and that the universe rewards those who help themselves. It's a strong belief system for Brittney in that she doesn't believe anything happens to her randomly. And, even if something happens to her that's out of her control, Brittney feels confident that she has the power to do something about it. Playing the victim is not in the cards for her: "I'm the driver of my happiness and my success. Even though I do think the universe rewards me all the time."

I asked Brittney how she sees the situation when something bad unexpectedly happens to her. "I feel like my attitude of gratitude helps me in bad situations," she says, "because there are a lot of people who say, 'Why me?!', and I say, 'Why not me? Why am I so special that I shouldn't get any hardships?' When I do have a hardship, I feel it's up to me to focus on what I can do about it. I think the more you learn, the more you can understand more people. The more hardships you go through, the more you can understand other people. I definitely think it's a blessing in disguise most of the time. Sometimes it's hard to see, but I try to focus on what I can learn from it."

When experiencing tough times, Brittney tries to connect with her spiritual beliefs. She has had many important people in her life pass away, and she pictures them with her. This technique has also helped her with her struggles with anxiety, which she says she doesn't experience as much anymore. So even if she's really struggling with whatever curve balls life has thrown at her, picturing her loved ones who have passed helps her get through the darkness. "If I was meant to get through it, I will. I know I'm very strong and can get through anything if I choose to. And if I'm not meant to get through it, well…either way, I'll be fine.

"I believe anybody can get through anything they choose to get through," Brittney continues. And if you start incorporating small habits, it will make a huge difference in your life if you keep those habits consistently. If you want to be better at eating or be healthier, it's not about having to wake up and completely change my life. It's more like, 'Today I'm going to have a healthy breakfast.' Baby steps. Consistently exercising those habits and building on them."

How do Brittney's family and friends cope with stress? Her husband is not spiritual, nor religious, but Brittney is spiritual. They are at each end of the belief spectrum. He believes life is precious and life is short, so we must make the most of it and be good to people. Brittney shares the same beliefs, but in a spiritual context in the sense that she believes she's in this life for a reason—to make a positive difference in people's lives—and that she'll be reunited with her loved ones who have already passed on. After Brittney's accident, her parents became more cognizant of how fragile life can be. It was such a traumatic event; they almost lost their daughter.

Brittney says her grandmother was an inspiration to her: "She showed me emotional and spiritual strength. I looked up to her."

And, fortunately, Brittney's friends are amazing and happy people. "I haven't met somebody with a disability who is unhappy," she says. "I know that sounds really strange. I've met people who are super high level quadriplegic who can't move anything but their neck, yet they are super happy. I have a lot of friends in wheelchairs, and we have the best time ever. We joke, we laugh, we always make light of things. Even though we sometimes say we want to make things better, we all think that we live beautiful lives."

If we look carefully, we can see that those dark moments we experience can teach us about empathy. If we can identify with them, they teach us to connect with others more easily. Those dark moments teach us to appreciate and cherish beauty and the happy times when times are good because we know the happy times won't last forever. But bad times don't last forever either. Our negative emotions, whether anxiety or irritability, can serve as a tool to remind us that we can and will get through the struggle, and that happiness is waiting on the other side. After every rainstorm, there will be sunshine.

Brittney doesn't think resilient people are immune to stress and negative emotions. "I think they just do it," she says. "I think resilient people are scared, but do it anyway. They do it even if they're afraid. They have the same negative emotions; they just choose to not focus on them and take that step."

Brittney feels the term *perseverance* has been misused in the mental health world. You can't just get over it (mental illness). It's easier said than done when someone says, "If only you're strong enough and pull up your boots, you will get over it." No matter how positive or strong one tries to be, depression and anxiety can sometimes overtake them. If the cause is something chemical, it's beyond anybody's control.

However, Brittney wants to add that sometimes you can get through it without becoming mentally unwell. Everybody's going to get frustrated, so don't succumb to it. No matter who you are or what circumstance you're in, you're going to be in situations that are trying. Don't let those situations define your journey. Remember that you're getting there instead of focusing on the frustrations of getting there.

Brittney relies on the memory of loved ones who have passed on as a tool to help her get through the difficult moments. She thinks of Blake (her friend who passed away while snowmobiling) a lot. His memory and their time together has been a source of encouragement, strength, and motivation for Brittney throughout all these years. "No matter what I'm experiencing in life, at least I am experiencing it. He died at 14, so his parents don't get to see his children; he doesn't get to have a family or do any of this stuff, or see the sunrise … simple stuff. I just think of all of the simple things I shouldn't take for granted because, at the end of the day, I'm here." Blake is Brittney's guardian angel.

I asked Brittney if she had any other words of wisdom she would like to share with others who may be struggling. "Trust your strength and your ability to problem solve," she says. "There were times, like when I was pregnant, that I was so scared. I didn't know what to do. Sometimes my husband actually had to have confidence for me at times. But no matter what you're going through, if you decide you're going to be happy or you're going to push through, you will! Trust yourself, trust in your own ability, trust in your talents, and trust that you have a purpose. Whatever it is, you're on this earth for a reason, not to just get frustrated and have a terrible life. Everybody was meant to have a beautiful life in some way or another."

Closing Remarks

I tell these stories from the voiceless because mental health and mental illness are stigmatized concepts. This present issue needs to be addressed by every town or city, so they can have a healthy future. If we stress the importance of mental health head-on now, this in turn may contribute to a decrease in addiction, homelessness, and poverty, since mental illness is often at the root of these societal issues. Healthy towns, cities, and countries need healthy citizens.

Mental health is a shared experience. It connects us to where we live, locally and globally. Mental health is indiscriminate of how new or established you are where you're living. It may not affect you directly, but it may affect you indirectly. We owe it to ourselves to help each other, and I believe this book provides a rich resource for opening up opportunities to collaborate and build partnerships with various Edmonton organizations and groups to encourage conversations about mental health and mental illness and debunk stereotypes surrounding these concepts.

Coming from a culturally marginalized community (Chinese), I see first-hand the stigma and stereotypes surrounding mental illness within my culture. As a writer of colour, it's even more important to me that this book contributes to the continuation of this dialogue in various communities of colour; mental health and mental illness can be stigmatized, or even a foreign concept, in these communities. I also hope to have this book translated into other languages, so communities of colour can understand these concepts and share in the stories of mental health experiences. These stories will become a rich part of Edmonton's history that will empower Edmontonians to value who they are and work towards a positive and healthy quality of life.

Equally important, as a step forward in speaking the Truth and working towards Reconciliation, as well as forging a new and respectful relationship between Indigenous and non-Indigenous Canadians, I hope this book will serve as an important vessel for sharing the Indigenous experience through Chevi Rabbit's and Shirley Rabbit's stories of discrimination, intergenerational trauma, and the residential school system. It will be a somber reminder of one of the darkest parts of Canada's history.

My initial intention for writing this book was to bring about change in the mental health or mental illness discourse and narrative by reassuring those who are struggling that they're not alone and to encourage them to seek help. From anybody. From anywhere. Just ask. That still is, and always will be, my intention.

What I didn't expect was how much the eight personal experiences shared within this book would change me—for the better, of course. Each of them opened up to me and trusted me to share an extremely vulnerable part of their lives, and I am forever deeply honoured. I know it wasn't easy for them to share their stories. But they did so because they want to help others. I was merely a vessel that held all of their struggles until it was time to share them with the world. Now is that time. My only regret is that I didn't write this book sooner. Like many others, I too have lost many loved ones to mental illness. This is not to say my book would have necessarily made a difference in their lives, or in anybody's life. But you never know whom the stories in this book will end up reaching out to. Even if just one of these eight stories touches just one struggling person, my personal joy will be indescribable.

I know I'm not the same person as I was before I wrote this book. I have taken so many things in my life for granted—guilty as charged, many times over. Every decision I now make, I make with positive intentions, with substance, and with meaning. Shirley, Chevi, Wei, Joy, Vivian, Brittney, Bailey, and Dan: I'm a better person today because of you. I can't say that I'm "there" yet, but I'll keep trying every minute of every day. Because of all of you, I am more cognizant of how my actions, words, and decisions will negatively or positively impact others and my own well-being.

In what ways? Well, for instance, for my niece's birthday, I donated food to the Edmonton Food Bank in her honour instead of buying her a gift or giving her money. I had never done this before, and she didn't quite understand it. But I hope she will one day. Also, I want to connect meaning to my book launch. During my book launch, I plan on fundraising, via the sale of my first and second books, to raise money for the purchase of the EMPWR Coats for the homeless in our city. To combat the butchering and unforgiving Edmonton winters, this coat is ideal for those who call the streets their home and are suffering from some form of mental illness. According to The Empowerment Plan website (empowermentplan.org), the EMPWR Coat is a water-resistant jacket that can transform into a sleeping bag or be worn as an over-the-shoulder bag when not in use.

And for my upcoming birthday—a very important milestone—I want to spend my special day helping others less fortunate. Partying seems so frivolous and superficial when there are so many who are suffering. I haven't confirmed my plans for that yet, but it's something that I wouldn't have thought about prior to meeting these eight brave souls and hearing their stories.

When I was interviewing Shirley, I shared with her my paralyzing phobia of highway driving. She said that she had been in an accident once, but she refused to let the fear of driving again get the best of her. That simple comment alone got me through three recent highway drives—two down to Calgary, and one to the town of Devon to see the Botanical Gardens. There was a lot of self-talk, deep breathing, and clammy hands involved as I white-knuckled my way to these destinations. But I overcame my decades-long fear, and that's all that matters. Thank you, Shirley. I feel like the luckiest girl in the world to have been born in the right place at the right time and to have met the people I've met throughout my life (whether the experience was good or bad). I feel so awake it's indescribable. I hope I continue to live my life in this state.

Each of these stories was heavy for me. I had to space out the stories when I was interviewing and writing because each and every single one affected me deeply. The pain in each one was heavy. I didn't realize how much that would affect me, but it did. It made me re-evaluate my problems with less drama and intensity and with more gratitude. I hope I don't sound like I'm complaining, because that's not at all my intention. If anything, each of the personal stories in this book taught me to be more empathetic and to understand that everyone (even the ones who look like they've got it all together) has a story. We're all looking to make the right decisions, all trying to meet the needs and desires of our families, all trying to know ourselves, all looking for an environment that uplifts us. We all share this human experience.

If you have a story you feel may help others, share it. None of us have to go through our struggles alone. Everyone is experiencing some degree of challenge. We need to help each other because we're all vulnerable to life's challenges. And, when we help each other, how can the winds of life break us? They won't; the most they will do is bend us and make us stronger than we were before.

No one is immune to the curve balls of life. These curve balls are indiscriminate, and you're not an exception. All stories are unique, and all stories are worthy. True stories are full of messy complications. They don't end in half-an-hour, tied up in a neat, shiny bow. Share your story. And when you do, embrace all the pain and all the ghosts that come with it. You're one of the bravest people already just by taking that first and most difficult step toward being heard.

You don't need to write a book about it (unless you want to). You can share it via a podcast, a rap song, a poem, a painting, a mime dance, a comic strip, or just with a good friend over a cup of tea on a Sunday afternoon. You never know who's hanging onto every word you say, and you could be helping someone else take that next step in getting help. Sometimes the risk of being stigmatized is worth it if it means forever changing just one person's life for the better.

Appendix

Questions for Interviewees

1. Can you tell us a little bit about yourself, a little bit of your background?

2. Can you tell us about a difficult incident in your life that really shook you to the fibres of your core?

3. Do you think your relationship with your friends and family helped you or made things worse in overcoming this difficult incident?

4. Do you think you have a positive view of yourself? Do you see yourself as a pretty confident person generally? Where do you get that? Or is confidence something you struggle with and need to work toward?

5. Are you someone who has the ability to control your feelings and impulses?

6. We all go through rough times, many times in our life. When you're going through rough times, do you think you have good problem-solving and communication skills, or do you normally keep things internalized and try to solve them on your own? Or do you seek external help and resources to help yourself?

7. Do you feel you're in control of your life most of the time? Or not at all?

8. When something bad unexpectedly happens, do you feel like a victim, or do you see the experience as an opportunity to learn and grow from, coming out of it as a different, stronger, and better person? Do you also see the experience as an opportunity to help others and/or as a blessing in disguise?

9. I try to read as many inspirational quotations as I can when I'm having a rough time. It helps me stay focused on what's important. How did you get through your tough time? Do you cope with stress in healthy ways? If not, how do you cope?

10. How do your friends and family cope with stress? What are your thoughts on how they cope?

11. Do you think it's also important to have negative emotions, such as emotional struggles, as a sign of perseverance, learning experiences, and spiritual growth?

12. What are your thoughts when I say this: Resilient people are immune to stress and negative emotions! Do you think this is true?

13. The word *perseverance* shows up in a lot of business literature. Do you think this concept is also vital to mental health? If so, why and how? If not, why don't you think so?

14. Keep pushing, keep trying, and don't succumb to frustration! What does this statement mean to you?

15. We can't be resilient all the time. What thought processes or tools do you use to help you get through the most difficult of times?

16. What words of wisdom or advice can you share with others going through a rough time in their lives?

Bibliography

American Psychological Association. (2019, May 2). Perseverance toward life goals can fend off depression, anxiety, panic disorders: Looking on the bright side also acts as a safeguard, according to 18-year study. *ScienceDaily*. Retrieved from www.sciencedaily.com/releases/2019/05/190502100852.htm.

Canadian Mental Health Association. (2016, February 27). Mental Health for Life. Retrieved from https://cmha.ca/documents/mental-health-for-life.

Centre for Addiction and Mental Health. (2019). Stigma: Understanding The Impact of Prejudice and Discrimination. Retrieved from https://www.camh.ca/en/health-info/guides-and-publications/stigma.

Cherry, Kendra. (2019, August 17). The Importance of Resilience. *Verywell mind.* Retrieved from https://www.verywellmind.com/what-is-resilience-2795059.

Davey, Graham C.L. (2013, August 20). Why We Worry. Mental Health and Stigma: Mental Health Symptoms Are Still Viewed As Threatening And Uncomfortable. *Psychology Today.* Retrieved from https://www.psychologytoday.com/ca/blog/why-we-worry/201308/mental-health-stigma.

Estroff Marano, Hara. (2003, May 1). The Art of Resilience: Research on resilience breaks down the myth that a troubled childhood leaves us emotionally crippled as an adult. *Psychology Today.* Retrieved from https://www.psychologytoday.com/ca/articles/200305/the-art-resilience.

About the author

Nancy Ng was born in Maracay, Aragua, Venezuela. Nancy is also the author of *No, Really, Where Are You From?: Personal Stories of Chinese Identity Retention and Loss* (2012). She has written and produced a play, *The Yellow Peril*, for the 2003 Edmonton Fringe Festival. She graduated from the University of Alberta with a BA in Sociology, and from Carleton University, with an MA in Sociology. Nancy currently makes her home in Canada, and she is most happiest when reading and climbing…just not at the same time.

Website: NancyNgSite.com
Twitter: @Iwillclimb

Manufactured by Amazon.ca
Bolton, ON